DATE DUE

9-24	
SEP 1 1 2009	
NOV 0 4 2009	
JAN 2 5 2012	

THE ENCYCLOPEDIA OF
U.S. Presidential
Elections

David C. Saffell, Ph.D.
Ohio Northern University
General Editor

Richard C. Remy, Ph.D.
Professor Emeritus, The Ohio State University
Adviser

Franklin Watts
A Division of Scholastic Inc.

New York Toronto London Auckland Sydney
Mexico City New Delhi Hong Kong
Danbury, Connecticut

DEVELOPED, DESIGNED, AND PRODUCED BY
BOOK BUILDERS LLC

Images by permission of: Bettman/Corbis: cover *top right*, cover *bottom left*; American Presidents Portraits commissioned by **C-SPAN** for their 20th anniversary video series: 8, 10, 12, 14, 17, 19, 21, 23, 25, 27, 29, 31, 33, 35, 37, 39, 41, 42, 44, 47, 49, 51, 53, 56, 58, 60, 62, 64, 66, 68, 70, 71, 73, 75, 77, 79, 81, 83, 85, 87, 89, 92, 94, 96, 99, 102, 104, 107, 109, 111, 113, 115, 117, 119; **Duke University,** Rare Book, Manuscript, & Special Collections Library: 100; **FDR Library:** 84; courtesy of **Darrell J. Kozlowski:** 8, 92, 104, 106, 112 *top right*, 114; **Library of Congress:** cover *bottom center,* cover *bottom right*, 66; **The Ronald Reagan Presidential Library:** 112 *bottom left*; **St. Louis Mercantile Library at the University of Missouri-St. Louis:** cover *top left,* 90. Interior design by D. Quintana and cover design by J. Glick for Book Builders LLC.

Every effort has been made to obtain permission to use copyrighted material. The publishers would appreciate errors or omissions being brought to their attention.

Library of Congress Cataloging-in-Publication Data

The encyclopedia of U.S. presidential elections / David C. Saffell, general editor.
  p. cm. — (Watts reference)
  Summary: Chronicles the candidates, issues, platforms, campaign slogans,
  and influences of presidential elections in the United States from 1789
  through 2000.
  Includes bibliographical references and index.
  ISBN 0-531-12051-1
  1. Presidents—United States—Election—History—Encyclopedias,
  Juvenile. 2. United States—Politics and government—Encyclopedias,
  Juvenile. [1. Presidents—Election—History—Encyclopedias. 2.
  Elections—History—Encyclopedias. 3. Politics,
  Practical—History—Encyclopedias. 4. United States—Politics and
  government—Encyclopedias.] I. Title: Encyclopedia of U.S. presidential
  elections. II. Title: Encyclopedia of United States presidential
  elections. III. Saffell, David C., 1941- IV. Series.

E176.1 .E48 2004
324.973'003—dc21

                                        2002038009

Contents

Note to the Reader

The first American presidential election was held in 1789. Since 1792, one has been held every four years. Will the next presidential election be a cliff-hanger? What campaign strategies help the candidates? Do smear tactics work? These questions–and more–have been asked since 1792.

In colonial America, only people who owned property or paid taxes could vote. By the 1830s, nearly all white men could vote. Later, African Americans, and then women, gained the right to vote. Now nearly all Americans over the age of 18 are eligible to cast their ballots for the person who holds the most powerful political position in the world–the president of the United States of America.

This encyclopedia will guide you through the election of each president from George Washington to George W. Bush. You will read about the candidates, the main issues at the time of each election, and how campaigns were run. You will learn why some candidates won and others lost.

As we know from the very close presidential election in 2000, when there was less than 0.4 percent difference in votes for Al Gore and George W. Bush in five states, each person's vote is important in all elections. For democracy to work well, we need to know what the candidates stand for. Then we must turn out to vote. Who knows, maybe a future president or vice president is in your class.

—David C. Saffell, *General Editor*

How to Use This Book

The entries in *The Encyclopedia of U.S. Presidential Elections* are arranged in chronological order, beginning with the first election of 1789. They identify and explain each of the candidates, the issues, the campaigns, and the results of every election.

Most entries in the encyclopedia contain cross-references. These are words or phrases in SMALL CAPITAL LETTERS that point you to related elections discussed in a separate entry in the encyclopedia. You will find helpful **bold-faced words** that are defined in the Glossary, located near the back of the book. Also throughout the encyclopedia are special features, which appear in lightly colored boxes, that profile people who were important to each president and his election or put a spotlight on the important events that influenced the election.

—Darrell J. Kozlowski, *Editor*

Note to the Educator

The *Encyclopedia of U.S. Presidential Elections* provides your students convenient access to information about the events, issues, and personalities in every presidential election from 1789 to 2000. Each entry also places the election in the broader context of American society at the time.

To help bring history alive to young researchers, special features profile first ladies, vice presidents, cabinet members, and other people who made significant contributions to American life or influenced an election. Other features highlight memorable issues of a campaign.

The encyclopedia will help students acquire specific information about elections and presidential candidates in order to write reports about American history and politics. As we know, the results of many presidential elections, such as those of 1860, 1896, 1932, and 1968, have deeply affected the course of American history. With good resources, students can understand how nineteenth- and twentieth-century elections remain relevant in the twenty-first century.

The historic 2000 presidential election led to calls for electoral reform. As each new election approaches, this encyclopedia will serve to help young people who are interested in learning how campaigns are run. Building on that interest, we have the opportunity to help students become better-informed adults, who will actively participate in the political process.

—David C. Saffell, *General Editor*

How Presidential Elections Work

The framers of the United States Constitution considered several ways to elect the president. Some wanted the president chosen by Congress, others wanted the selection to be made by state legislatures. Only a few wanted the people to vote directly for the president.

After much debate, the framers agreed to create an Electoral College in which the people would vote for electors, who would then choose the president. The framers believed that the electors, who often were state legislators, would make wiser choices than the people.

The number of electors each state has in the Electoral College is equal to its total number of United States representatives and senators. Since each state has two senators and at least one representative, every state has at least three electoral votes.

According to the way the Constitution was originally written, the candidate who won a majority of all the electoral votes would be president and the runner-up would be vice president. If no candidate received a majority of the total votes, which was what the framers thought was likely to happen, then the House of Representatives would choose the president from among the top three candidates.

As political parties developed, changes in how the Electoral College works were made. For example, in the election of 1800 the Democratic-Republican party electors intended to vote for Thomas Jefferson for president and Aaron Burr for vice president. Because the electors did not indicate who was to be president and who was to be vice president, Jefferson and Burr tied. The House of Representatives had to select the president. The confusion led to the ratification of the Twelfth Amendment (1804), which calls for the names of presidential and vice presidential candidates to appear on separate ballots.

In the 1800s most presidential candidates did not personally campaign. Sometimes they made a few speeches; often, supporters came to the candidate's home, from which he gave a speech. By the middle of the twentieth century, presidential campaigns had changed greatly. Traveling first by train, then by car, and now by airplane, candidates crisscross the country and speak to huge crowds, thus reaching more voters.

In the 1950s and 1960s, television *really* changed campaigning. The first televised presidential debate was held in 1960. Because more voters than ever were able to see the candidates, many experts believe that the 1960 debates helped elect Democrat John F. Kennedy in a very close contest.

With the increasing impact of television, candidates discovered that often-times "sound bites," or short statements, could sway voters. Candidates and their supporters found that running short television ads attacking their opponents were often effective, but buying television time is expensive. As a result, candidates in recent years have devoted more time and effort to raising funds to buy air time. To help reduce the influence of money in presidential elections, Congress approved government financing, which began with the 1976 presidential election.

The ELECTION OF 2000 was an overtime thriller and will likely be discussed for years to come. Interest in the campaign had been fairly low, but the excitement came on election day and in the weeks that followed. The election was decided only after counts, recounts, state court rulings, and finally a decision by the United States Supreme Court. For the first time since 1888, the winner of the popular vote was not elected president. How could this happen? Does this mean we should get rid of the Electoral College?

On the night of the election, it became clear that in several states the popular vote was so close that no one could determine which candidate would win the state's electoral votes. At first the television networks "called" Florida for George W. Bush, but later in the evening changed their prediction to Al Gore. By the early morning, no one knew who had won the election because Florida, with 25 electoral votes, was by far the largest state in which the winner was in doubt. It was obvious that the outcome in Florida would decide who would be the next president.

Votes continued to be counted and recounted in Florida well into December—weeks after the election. Finally, the United States Supreme Court overruled the Florida supreme court on the issue of continuing the recount. With no more time to keep recounting, the Florida vote count stood. Bush won the state by 537 popular votes. With Florida's 25 votes, he had a total of 271 electoral votes with 270 required for victory. More than 105 million votes were cast for president, but the election was decided by a fraction of 1 percent of those votes. Interestingly, most Americans accepted the results with little complaint and gave President Bush their support even before the tragic events of September 11, 2001.

Electoral College votes are awarded on a state-by-state basis. The candidate who wins the most votes in a state gets all that state's electoral votes. This means it is possible to win the national popular vote, as Al Gore did by about 500,000 votes, but lose the vote in the Electoral College. That situation troubles many people. Some government officials have called for the Electoral College to be replaced by a direct national vote.

Supporters of the Electoral College responded that it worked well in 2000. They point out that the system forces candidates to pay attention to small states, such as New Mexico and New Hampshire, where the 2000 vote was very close. Because the presidential vote is state-by-state, it means any recounting will be done only in a few states. Supporters point to how time-consuming and complicated it would have been to have had a national recount, rather than just a Florida recount, in 2000.

Although confusion remains regarding how ballots were counted in Florida and opinions differ about the need to reform the Electoral College, it is clear that Americans have seen how important a few votes can be in electing the president of the United States.

Presidential election campaigns may, at times, appear disorganized or confused. They are frequently colorful, noisy, chaotic, and sometimes nasty. Candidates often make hard-to-keep promises to earn votes. Their campaign managers try different strategies and approaches. And if one campaign tactic does not work, they will try another to win the voters' attention—and ultimately the presidency. Yet, despite all this, every four years the winner pulls together a transition team to guide the orderly change of administration and to smoothly continue the straightforward business of governing. Perhaps former New York governor Mario Cuomo best indicated the difference between campaigning and governing, noting: "You campaign in poetry. You govern in prose."

—David C. Saffell, *General Editor*

Electoral Votes, Based on the 2000 Census

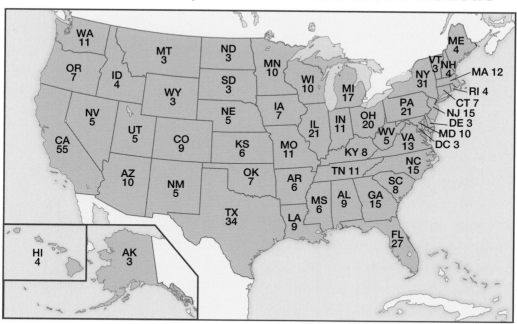

According to the Constitution, each state, including the District of Columbia, is entitled to at least three electors. These are the people who perform the formal duty of voting for their state. However, the number of a state's electors may change based on the population count of the most recent census.

Election of 1789

The Candidates The first presidential election was unique. George Washington, commander in chief of the Continental Army, had defeated the British and secured the nation's independence, but he did not want the presidency. Although he preferred to retire to his beloved estate at Mount Vernon, Virginia, Americans looked to Washington to lead the young nation through its early years. He was so admired that no one considered challenging him.

Political parties did not yet play a part in elections, but Washington made it clear that he wanted John Adams of Massachusetts as vice president. Adams had served the country as a

> ● "I walk on
> ● untrodden
> ● [new]
> ● ground . . ."
> ● —*Washington, early in his first term*

▲ Washington was respected and trusted by all the people.

revolutionary patriot, coauthor of the Declaration of Independence, and diplomat to Europe.

The Issues After the Revolutionary War, the nation was governed under a plan known as the **Articles of Confederation**, which established a weak central government with little authority. Economic problems, a huge national debt, and riots troubled the country. Many leaders from the Revolutionary War (1775–1783), including Alexander Hamilton of New York, Benjamin Franklin of

One precedent that President Washington established was the Cabinet—a group made up of the heads of government departments that the president consults. The Cabinet is not mentioned in the Constitution. Yet every president since Washington has consulted with his Cabinet members. Washington appointed four men to the first Cabinet—Thomas Jefferson as secretary of state, Alexander Hamilton as secretary of the treasury, Henry Knox as secretary of war, and Edmund Randolph as attorney general.

A commemorative silver dollar celebrates the 200th anniversary of the United States Constitution in 1987.

Martha Washington (1731–1802), a wealthy widow with two children, married George Washington in 1759. As the first First Lady, Martha enjoyed entertaining and started several customs, including Friday afternoon parties for the women. She also began the practice of meeting with the public on New Year's Day, which continued until 1931. She probably gave some of her own silver to the new government to be minted into the nation's first coins—silver five-cent pieces known as half-dismes [dimes].

Pennsylvania, and Washington himself, called for the nation's federal government to be strengthened.

As a result, delegates from 12 of the 13 states met in Philadelphia and crafted a new, stronger central government. The Constitution went into effect in June 1788 when New Hampshire became the ninth state to **ratify**, or approve, it. By July of that year, all the states except North Carolina and Rhode Island had approved it. Thus, organizing and running the new government as set up under the Constitution, the document that serves as the supreme law of the land, was the key issue facing the young nation.

The Campaign Washington did not campaign for office. He knew that as the first president, he would set the example for all chief executives to follow. The American people trusted Washington and felt sure he would not abuse the powers of the presidency.

The Election In the first four presidential elections, electors were required to cast their ballots for two candidates. The candidate with the highest number of votes became president and the one with the second-highest number became vice president. This system, set up by the Constitution, did not work well once political parties arose. The Twelfth Amendment, ratified in 1804, called for each elector to choose two candidates, one for president and one for vice president. This electoral system is still in use today.

On April 6, 1789, the Senate officially counted the electoral votes. While Washington had won all 69 votes to become president, Adams had won only 34 and was made vice president. On April 30, 1789, George Washington took the first oath of office: "I do solemnly swear that I will faithfully execute the office of president of the United States, and will, to the best of my ability, preserve, protect, and defend the Constitution of the United States. . . ." All presidents since that day have taken the same oath as Washington. *See also* ELECTION OF 1792 (WASHINGTON); ELECTION OF 1796 (JOHN ADAMS); ELECTION OF 1800 (JEFFERSON).

Election of 1792

George Washington ⊙ George Washington planned to retire after his first term, but James Madison, Thomas Jefferson, and others urged him to stay in office for another four years. Washington then changed his mind for the good of the nation.

The Candidates As in 1789, Washington was unopposed for the presidency. John Adams, Washington's vice president, ran as well.

During this election, political leaders were beginning to side with one candidate over another—the start of **political parties**. Although Washington opposed political parties, he tended to side with those who favored a strong central government—the **Federalists**. John Adams and Alexander Hamilton were among its leaders. Those who

▲ Washington established the presidential tradition of serving two terms, which lasted until 1940.

> "North and South will hang together if they have you to hang on."
>
> —*Thomas Jefferson, encouraging Washington to run for a second term*

favored a weak central government, but stronger state governments, were at first known as **Anti-Federalists**. Later they became known as **Democratic-Republicans**. Two of their leaders were Thomas Jefferson and James Madison. Some Anti-Federalists rallied around George Clinton, a former New York governor, to oppose Adams for vice president.

Secretary of the Treasury Alexander Hamilton quickly put together a much-needed economic plan that included establishing a national bank. But Washington's secretary of state, Thomas Jefferson, opposed the bank because the new Constitution did not specifically permit the government to set up a bank. In turn, Hamilton argued that Article I, Section 18, of the Constitution gave the government the power "to make all laws necessary and proper" to carry out its responsibilities. Washington listened to both cabinet members but eventually agreed with Hamilton and signed the bill establishing the bank.

The Issues Among the chief issues during the election of 1796 was the financial plan of Alexander Hamilton, a plan that had become law during Washington's first term. Hamilton's plan had four main parts: (1) the funding of all debts left from the Revolution; (2) new and higher **excise taxes**; (3) the creation of a national bank; and (4) **tariffs**, or taxes, on imported goods. Northern states, which had larger debts and more industry, tended to favor Hamilton's plan. Southern states, which had smaller debts and were mostly agricultural, opposed the plan. Thomas Jefferson spoke for the southern states and small farmers.

Jefferson believed that the young United States should remain a rural, agricultural nation. He trusted the people and believed that they should control the government. Jefferson favored a weak national government.

Alexander Hamilton (1755?–1804) was born in the British West Indies and moved to New Jersey in 1772. During the American Revolution, he served under General George Washington. Later he authored some of the *Federalist Papers*, urging ratification of the Constitution. In 1789, at the age of 34, Hamilton became the first secretary of the treasury. His financial plans put the nation on a sound footing. When Aaron Burr and Thomas Jefferson received the same number of electoral votes in the election of 1800, Hamilton opposed Burr and help swing votes to Jefferson. Later, when Burr ran for New York governor, Hamilton worked hard to defeat him, for it was believed that Burr had conspired against the United States. Burr challenged Hamilton to a duel and wounded him in Weehawken, New Jersey, on the morning of July 11, 1804. Hamilton died the following day.

In contrast, Hamilton saw the future United States as a nation of cities and industry. He believed the common people alone were not able to govern themselves, and he favored a strong national government run by well-educated men of property.

The Campaign Neither Washington nor Adams campaigned. Rather than attack Washington, the Anti-Federalists took aim at Vice President Adams. They claimed he supported **monarchy**, or rule by a king, opposed democratic ideas, and favored the rich. Adams, a brilliant and serious man, had a sharp temper and did not make friends easily. Thus he became an easy target of criticism.

The Election Once again Washington received all of the electoral votes—132 total. Vice President Adams received 77. Anti-Federalist electors cast 50 votes for George Clinton, not enough to win the vice presidency. *See also* ELECTION OF 1789 (WASHINGTON); ELECTION OF 1796 (JOHN ADAMS); ELECTION OF 1800 (JEFFERSON).

Election of 1796

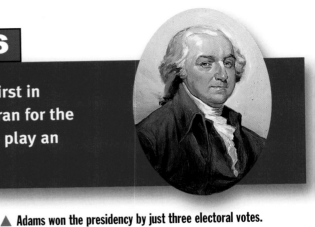

John Adams ✪ The election of 1796 was the first in which candidates with very different views ran for the office. As a result, political parties began to play an important role in the election process.

The Candidates In the early days of the nation, presidential and vice-presidential candidates were not selected by political party conventions, as they are today. Oftentimes candidates were chosen by key members of Congress in a meeting known as a **caucus**.

Vice President John Adams was known throughout the country, was trusted by President Washington, and had the support of most **Federalists**. It became clear that he would be the Federalist candidate. In addition to his experience as vice president, Adams's service to the nation went back to the days before the American Revolution. He had been a delegate to the Continental Congress, which had declared independence from Great Britain, and was a coauthor of the Declaration of Independence. He also served as minister to France and later to Great Britain. In addition, he was honest, dedicated to the country, and an expert in government. Thomas Pinckney, the successful diplomat who secured

▲ Adams won the presidency by just three electoral votes.

● **"The Father of**
● **American**
● **Independence"**
● *—Nickname for John Adams*
●

Abigail Adams (1744–1818) had little formal education, but she was well versed in literature and the arts. She married John Adams in 1764. John was often away from home as he pursued his political career, and Abigail efficiently ran the family farm in Quincy, Massachusetts. In one of her famous letters to her husband, she urged John to support American independence and the abolition of slavery. During the Constitutional Convention, she asked John to "remember the ladies." She was the first First Lady to live in the yet unfinished White House, where she had to hang laundry in the East Room. She was the mother of the sixth president, John Quincy Adams.

the Treaty with Spain (1795) under President Washington, became his running mate.

Those who opposed the Federalists, soon to be known as **Democratic-Republicans**, rallied around Thomas Jefferson, Washington's former secretary of state, as their presidential candidate. Jefferson, the chief author of the Declaration of Independence, also had vast government experience. He, too, served as a minister to France. Democratic-Republican leaders planned to elect Aaron Burr, a political leader from New York, as vice president.

The Issues The 1794 Jay Treaty with Great Britain, which had narrowly passed in the Senate, was the main issue in the Election of 1796. The Federalists favored the treaty, though it did not recognize American **neutrality**, the practice of not taking sides in a war or conflict. In addition, the treaty did not address the issue of **impressment**, the British practice of boarding American ships and forcing American seamen to serve in the British navy. The Democratic-Republicans criticized the Jay Treaty as pro-British and insulting to the United States.

The Campaign None of the candidates campaigned. However, the campaign was fought across the country in pamphlets, newspapers, and in letters. **Mudslinging** and insults, often part of today's elections, started in 1796. Federalists claimed Jefferson was an atheist, a person who does not believe in God, and that he would bring the terror of the French Revolution to the United States. In turn, Democratic-Republicans called Adams a monarchist who would make himself king, and they claimed he favored the rich. They also attacked Washington's strong role in suppressing the Whiskey Rebellion, a farmers' uprising against federal taxes, as a threat to liberty.

The Election Alexander Hamilton disliked Adams and tried to get Thomas Pinckney elected instead. He suggested that the electors from Pinckney's home state of South Carolina vote only for Pinckney and withhold their vote for Adams. In this way, he hoped that Pinckney would win more votes than Adams and become president. Rumors of this scheme leaked out, however. In the end, Adams won most of the votes of the northern states and Jefferson carried most of the southern states. Adams received 71 votes to Jefferson's 68, Pinckney's 59, and Burr's 30.

As a result of this election, the nation's two top leaders were members of different political parties. Adams, a Federalist, was president, and Jefferson, a Democratic-Republican, was vice president. The rise of political parties showed that the Constitution's instructions for how electors voted needed to be changed. But this change would not come until 1804. *See also* ELECTION OF 1792 (WASHINGTON); ELECTION OF 1800 (JEFFERSON); ELECTION OF 1804 (JEFFERSON).

Election **of 1800**

✪ The election of 1800 was a rematch between the candidates of 1796, but with very different results. This election reinforced the need to amend the Constitution and change the way electors voted.

The Candidates John Adams, as the **incumbent** president, easily became the **Federalist** candidate. For his running mate, the Federalists chose Charles C. Pinckney of South Carolina, brother of earlier Federalist candidate Thomas Pinckney, lawyer and diplomat.

As in 1796, the **Democratic-Republicans** looked to Virginian Thomas Jefferson as their presidential candidate. And again they chose Aaron Burr of New York to be vice president.

The Issues Since his election in 1796, Adams had guided the nation through difficult times. Most of his administration was devoted to trying to keep peace with France. The leaders of the bloody French Revolution wanted the United States to join them in their war against Britain. The young nation was unprepared for war and refused. Also much of the nation's income came from trade with Britain. In return the French stopped American ships at sea, searched for goods headed to Britain, and threatened to hang any American sailors they captured on British ships.

Late in 1797, Adams sent a delegation to France to try to resolve the growing crisis. The French government, however, demanded a bribe from the Americans before they would be allowed to meet with the French minister. Adams was outraged, but kept the news secret. He was going to ask Congress for a declaration of war,

> • "We are all
> • Republicans,
> • we are all
> • Federalists."
>
> —*Thomas Jefferson,*
> *First Inaugural Address,*
> *March 4, 1801*

▲ Jefferson's election in 1800 was the first time in history that power passed peacefully from one political party to another.

but he realized that the nation was too weak. He instead asked Congress to allow American merchant ships to arm themselves and to create a navy. The Democratic-Republicans strongly opposed these and other war preparations. However, after Adams announced the French demands, most of the country rallied around him. "Millions for defense, but not one cent for tribute" became the nation's cry. An undeclared war with France began.

Despite Adams's public support, some Democratic-Republican newspapers continued to criticize him and the federal government. The Federalist-controlled Congress passed two laws to silence these critics—the Alien and Sedition Acts. Democratic-Republicans opposed these laws and claimed they violated the **Bill of Rights**.

In 1799 Adams stunned both Federalists and Democratic-Republicans when he proposed to try again to establish diplomatic relations with France. Under Adams's leadership, three diplomats were sent to France. By September 1800, just before the election, a new treaty had been signed and the threat of full-scale war declined. Some Federalists feared that Adams had doomed his reelection hopes.

The Campaign During the campaign, none of

Aaron Burr (1756–1836) was a New York lawyer and politician of great ambition. He quickly rose through the ranks of the Democratic-Republicans, becoming state attorney general and then a United States senator. But many people, Federalists and Democratic-Republicans alike, did not trust Burr. Even as vice president, Burr fell out of favor with President Jefferson.

Vice President Burr then decided to run for governor of New York. Fellow New Yorker Alexander Hamilton, who was suspicious of Burr, campaigned to defeat him. Burr challenged Hamilton to a duel. Burr took careful aim, fired, and mortally wounded Hamilton. An outcast, Burr fled to Philadelphia where he began to hatch a strange plot. To this day no one knows the plot's details, for Burr told several different versions. It likely centered on creating a huge empire that would include Spanish Mexico, the Louisiana Territory, and the states west of the Appalachian Mountains. James Wilkinson, governor of the Louisiana Territory and a fellow conspirator, betrayed Burr. When the plot came to light, Burr was arrested and in 1807 he was brought to trial. Chief Justice John Marshall applied a strict constitutional definition of treason—the betraying of one's country. Marshall insisted that conviction was possible only "on the testimony of two witnesses to the . . . act or on open confession in Court." Burr was acquitted and fled to France. He later returned to the United States to be with his only daughter. Sadly, as she sailed to meet him, her ship was lost at sea. Burr spent the rest of his life in New York City.

the candidates traveled or made speeches. Again the nation's journalists praised those candidates they favored and sharply criticized those they opposed. The Federalists attacked Jefferson as an atheist. They claimed that if Jefferson was elected, religion would be destroyed.

The Democratic-Republicans attacked Adams as a monarchist, who would try to become king if he were reelected. They severely criticized Adams for the undeclared war with France, even though the worst of the threat had passed. Adams's opponents strongly complained that the hated Alien and Sedition Acts destroyed the nation's liberty and violated the First Amendment.

Adams's fellow Federalist, Alexander Hamilton, was perhaps more critical of Adams than were the Democratic-Republicans. As Hamilton's dislike for Adams had grown over the past four years, he worked to defeat Adams. Hamilton tried to convince other Federalist leaders to stop supporting Adams. When they refused, he circulated letters and pamphlets claiming that Adams was unfit to continue in office. The lies about Adams had the desired effect.

The Election The well-organized Democratic-Republicans influenced their electors to vote for Jefferson and Burr. The Federalists, divided between those who favored Adams and the followers of Hamilton, split their votes. As a result, Jefferson and Burr tied at 73 votes each. Adams came in third with 65 votes. Charles Pinckney received 64 votes.

Because of the tie between Jefferson and Burr, the House of Representatives—voting by states—had to decide who would be president, as the Constitution requires. In the House, the Democratic-Republicans controlled 8 of the 16 state delegations—one short of a majority. On the first **ballot**, Jefferson received these eight votes and Burr received six votes from Federalist-controlled delegations. Because two states could not agree on a candidate, they were unable to cast their votes. This deadlock continued through 35 additional ballots.

Finally the efforts of Hamilton, as a leader of the Federalists, brought about Jefferson's victory. Hamilton, who had little admiration for Jefferson, believed that Burr was dishonest, selfish, and ambitious. He persuaded some Federalist House members to withhold their votes from Burr. This enabled Jefferson to receive a majority of the state delegations on the thirty-sixth ballot. On February 17, 1801, a little more than two weeks before Inauguration Day, Jefferson was declared president. Burr became vice president.

Because political power passed peacefully from the Federalists to the Democratic-Republicans, Jefferson often referred to his election as the "Revolution of 1800." Indeed, the principles set up by the Constitution endured despite the intrigues and **mudslinging** of the campaign.

This election and the election of 1796 led to the adoption of the Twelfth Amendment in 1804. Previously under the Constitution, electors voted for "two persons" without specifying who was to be president and who was to be vice president. With the ratification of the Twelfth Amendment, electors were required to cast one vote for president and one vote for vice president, on separate ballots. This amendment recognized the role of political parties in America. *See also* ELECTION OF 1796 (JOHN ADAMS); ELECTION OF 1804 (JEFFERSON).

Martha Jefferson (1748–1782) was widowed with one son when she married Thomas Jefferson in 1772. She and Jefferson had six children, but only two lived more than two years. Little is known about Martha Jefferson's early years, and there are no known portraits of her. Letters indicate that she was a talented piano player and that she kept the accounts at Jefferson's estate, Monticello. Upon her death, Jefferson was so upset that he refused to leave his room for three weeks. He never remarried. Because Jefferson was a widower when he entered the White House, his oldest daughter, Martha Jefferson Randolph, frequently acted as hostess for the president.

Election of 1804

Thomas Jefferson ✪ Jefferson was overwhelmingly reelected in 1804. He received 162 electoral votes to the Federalist candidate's 14.

▲ Jefferson's second term started on a positive note—peace and prosperity.

The Candidates As the election of 1804 approached, the nation was prosperous and at peace. The **Democratic-Republican caucus** easily named Thomas Jefferson as their choice for president. For vice president, they chose New York governor George Clinton, dropping the disgraced Aaron Burr.

The weakened **Federalists** did not officially name any candidates. Instead they recommended Charles C. Pinckney for president and Rufus King for vice president. Charles C. Pinckney, brother of earlier Federalist candidate Thomas Pinckney, had served in the American Revolution, had been a delegate to the Constitutional Convention, a senator from New York, and minister to Great Britain. Rufus King also served at the Constitutional Convention, was a New York senator, and an envoy to Britain.

The Issues Jefferson's first term had been very successful. He worked with Congress to repeal the hated Alien and Sedition Acts, which had been passed to

> ● **"The Father of the Declaration of Independence"**
> ● —Nickname of Thomas Jefferson

control criticism of the government, and he cut the size of the army and navy, thus reducing taxes. In 1803, he achieved his greatest accomplishment—the purchase of the Louisiana Territory from France for about $15 million. With this acquisition, Jefferson doubled the size of the nation and secured the use of the Mississippi River for western farmers. He also added the port city of New Orleans to the nation, thus ensuring the free passage of western crops and goods to overseas markets. Today, the vast land area of the original Louisiana Territory includes all or parts of the states of Louisiana, Arkansas, Missouri, Iowa, Minnesota, Texas, Oklahoma, Kansas, Nebraska, South Dakota, North Dakota, Colorado, Wyoming, and Montana.

Jefferson was popular throughout most of the country. John Randolph of Virginia wrote, "Never was

George Clinton (1739–1812) replaced Aaron Burr as the Democratic-Republican candidate for the vice presidency in 1804. Clinton was a powerful politician in New York and had served as the state's governor for six terms. In fact, Clinton's support had helped Burr advance his own political career. Clinton wanted to be president someday, and his New York backers tried to push him into the executive office in the election of 1808. Their support was not strong enough, however, and Clinton again became vice president under James Madison. Clinton died in office in 1812.

there an administration more brilliant than that of Mr. Jefferson up to this period."

The Campaign As in earlier campaigns, none of the candidates toured the country or made speeches. The **press**—newspapers, pamphlets, and other media—praised or attacked the candidates and attempted to influence voters' opinions.

Jefferson had never been popular in New England. In Massachusetts, where the Federalists controlled the state government, as well as the press and the clergy, the president was attacked with the same accusations as in the elections of 1796 and 1800. Once again he was called an atheist. They claimed he was about to bring the horrors of the French Revolution to America, that he destroyed the nation's military, and that he corrupted the courts. Yet all this political **mudslinging** had little effect. The people favored Jefferson, and his reelection was almost assured.

The Election Jefferson scored a great victory. He and vice presidential candidate Clinton won 162 **electoral votes**. The Federalists—Pinckney and King—won 14. Because the Twelfth Amendment had recently been added to the Constitution, the presidential and vice presidential candidates ran together as a **ticket**. In the future, they would almost always receive the same number of electoral votes. *See also* ELECTION OF 1796 (JOHN ADAMS); ELECTION OF 1800 (JEFFERSON).

Election of 1804		
States (Total Number of Electoral Votes)	*Thomas Jefferson (Democratic-Republican)*	*Charles C. Pinckney (Federalist)*
Connecticut (9)		9
Delaware (3)		3
Georgia (6)	6	
Kentucky (8)	8	
Maryland (11)	9	2
Massachussetts (19)	19	
New Hampshire (7)	7	
New Jersey (8)	8	
New York (19)	19	
North Carolina (14)	14	
Ohio (3)	3	
Pennsylvania (20)	20	
Rhode Island (4)	4	
South Carolina (10)	10	
Tennessee (5)	5	
Vermont (6)	6	
Virginia (24)	24	
Total (176)	**162**	**14**

Charles C. Pinckney, the Federalist candidate, received little support.

Election of 1808

James Madison ✪ James Madison, President Jefferson's friend and secretary of state, was his personal choice to succeed him. He easily won, receiving 122 electoral votes.

The Candidates Madison's contributions to the young United States included serving at the Constitutional Convention, authoring the Bill of Rights, and being Jefferson's secretary of state. Although Jefferson hand-picked Madison as his successor, not all members of the **Democratic-Republican** party favored Madison. New Yorkers favored Vice President George Clinton, and some Virginians wanted James Monroe. The

▲ Madison, like Jefferson and Washington, was from Virginia. Together with the fifth president, James Monroe, they are often called the "Virginia Dynasty."

- "The Father
- of the
- Constitution"
- —*Nickname for James Madison*

Democratic-Republicans rallied around Madison when it became known that he favored a strong stand in the ongoing **embargo** crisis of Jefferson's second term. The embargo, which kept American vessels in their ports, had hurt merchants and traders.

The **Federalist** party was in disarray and put up the same ticket as four years earlier— Charles C. Pinckney and Rufus King. The weakened Federalists provided little opposition to Madison.

James Madison, the fourth president, is known as the Father of the Constitution for three main reasons. First, Madison wrote most of the document. Second, he kept detailed notes of the Constitutional Convention. Most of what we know about the Convention comes from Madison's observations because the delegates' debates were closed to the public. Finally, Madison worked tirelessly for the new Constitution's approval. Along with Alexander Hamilton and John Jay, Madison wrote a series of essays supporting the Constitution. This collection of essays, known as *The Federalist,* is still studied today. In his home state of Virginia, Madison worked to win a narrow victory for the Constitution's approval.

The Issues The chief campaign issue was the embargo, an 1807 law passed by Congress that closed American ports to foreign ships and stopped American ships from carrying goods to Europe. France and Great Britain were again at war. Although the United States had declared its **neutrality**—not taking sides—both nations attacked U.S. ships. The British and French navies seized American merchant ships, took cargo, and practiced the **impressment**, or forced service, of sailors. Because Madison was Jefferson's secretary of state, he was deeply involved in the administration's policies.

Although Jefferson and Madison tried to negotiate with both nations, they were not successful. Jefferson and Madison hoped that the embargo would hinder Britain's and France's war efforts, causing them to stop interfering with American ships. Instead, the embargo hurt American shipping and industry. Crops and goods piled up on wharves waiting to be sent overseas. Exports decreased from about $108 million in 1807 to $22 million in 1808. The prosperity of Jefferson's first term had disappeared by late 1808, and, as the election neared, people called for the embargo to be lifted.

The Campaign The press, especially in New England, lashed out at Jefferson and the embargo. Federalists and Democratic-Republicans alike called for change. Some people not only called for a **repeal**, or end, of the Embargo Act but for war with Britain. The Federalist candidates—

Dolley Madison (1768–1849), a widow with two young sons, married James Madison in September 1794. Raised a Quaker, she was especially well educated for a woman of her times. Dolley loved entertaining and brought her high spirits into the White House when she became First Lady. She became the center of society in the nation's capital. During the War of 1812, when the British threatened Washington, she stayed in the White House long enough to save key documents and the famous portrait of George Washington by the artist Gilbert Stuart. Reduced to poverty after James Madison's death in 1836, she sold Montpelier, their Virginia estate. This enabled her to move back to Washington and once again become the center of society.

Pinckney and King—had no plan to offer and simply allowed the New England press to attack the administration.

The Election Despite the hardships caused by the embargo, the Democratic-Republicans were still popular, and the Federalists did not provide an attractive alternative. Madison and Clinton won 122 **electoral votes** to the Federalists' 47. Three days before Madison's inauguration, Jefferson signed the repeal of the Embargo Act, replacing it with a new law that permitted trade with any country except France and Britain. This law also allowed Madison to begin his presidency on a positive note. *See also* ELECTION OF 1800 (JEFFERSON); ELECTION OF 1804 (JEFFERSON); ELECTION OF 1812 (MADISON).

Election of 1812

James Madison ✪ James Madison was reelected a few months after the outbreak of the War of 1812. Many New Englanders opposed the war and supported DeWitt Clinton, the antiwar candidate from New York.

The Candidates Madison, who was very popular during his first term, was renominated by a congressional caucus. Elbridge Gerry, a former Massachusetts governor and a signer of the Declaration of Independence, was chosen for vice president.

Democratic-Republicans who opposed the war backed DeWitt Clinton, a long-time mayor of New York City and nephew of George Clinton, who was vice president during Jefferson's second term and Madison's first term. The **Federalists** backed Clinton rather than nominating a candidate of

▲ Most of Madison's second term was focused on the war with Great Britain.

- "Madison and War! Or Clinton and Peace."
  —*A New England Federalist's view of the campaign, 1812*

their own. Clinton's supporters selected Jared Ingersoll, a moderate Federalist from Pennsylvania, as their vice-presidential candidate.

The Issues Much of Madison's first term was centered on maintaining peace with Britain and France and assuring America's rights to trade freely with other countries. At first, he was popular with Democratic-Republicans and Federalists alike.

Elbridge Gerry (1744–1814) served in the First Continental Congress. In 1797, President John Adams sent him to France to help negotiate terms to prevent a full-scale war. Near the end of his term as Massachusetts governor, Gerry redrew congressional election districts to help the Democratic-Republicans keep control of the United States House of Representatives. The term *gerrymander* was coined by a critic who thought one of Gerry's new districts looked like a salamander. In the fall of 1814, Gerry collapsed and died on his way to the Senate. Today, gerrymandering refers to the drawing of election districts to favor one political party.

After the United States declared war on Britain on June 19, 1812, the War Hawks thought the nation would conquer Canada and win a quick victory. The British invaded Washington, D.C., in 1814 and burned the White House and several government buildings. During the British attack on Fort McHenry in Baltimore harbor, the Americans forced the British to retreat. The Treaty of Ghent, signed in December 1814, ended the war. The greatest American victory came after the peace treaty was signed. In January 1815, at the Battle of New Orleans, General Andrew Jackson inflicted a severe blow to the British, which made Jackson a national hero.

Despite his best efforts, by 1811 he was unable to keep the peace. Britain refused to honor its agreements with the United States, and young aggressive members of Congress, who became known as "War Hawks," clamored for war.

The Campaign As in earlier elections, the candidates did not campaign themselves. Clinton, the peace candidate, was supported by a **faction**, or subgroup, of Democratic-Republicans. Most New England Federalists quietly endorsed him, because they, too, opposed the war. The War Hawks, centered in the South and West, supported Madison and the war.

The Election Madison and Gerry won the election with 128 **electoral votes**, mostly from the South and West. Clinton and Ingersoll, with support from most of New England and New York, won 89 electoral votes. *See also* ELECTION OF 1804 (JEFFERSON); ELECTION OF 1808 (MADISON); ELECTION OF 1816 (MONROE).

Election of 1812

States (Total Number of Electoral Votes)	James Madison (Democratic-Republican)	DeWitt Clinton (Federalist)
Connecticut (9)		9
Delaware (4)		4
Georgia (8)	8	
Kentucky (12)	12	
Louisiana (3)	3	
Maryland (11)	6	5
Massachussetts (22)		22
New Hampshire (8)		8
New Jersey (8)		8
New York (29)		29
North Carolina (15)	15	
Ohio (8)	7*	
Pennsylvania (25)	25	
Rhode Island (4)		4
South Carolina (11)	11	
Tennessee (8)	8	
Vermont (8)	8	
Virginia (25)	25	
Total (218)	**128**	**89**

*One Ohio elector did not vote

Madison's political support was in the southern and western states.

Election of 1816

James Monroe ✪ James Monroe was the last Revolutionary War hero to be elected president. His terms as president were peaceful and prosperous and there were few political troubles.

The Candidates After the War of 1812 ended, the popularity of President Madison and the **Democratic-Republicans** soared. Madison, following the two-term tradition started by Washington, chose not to run again. The Democratic-Republicans selected James Monroe of Virginia as their candidate. Monroe was a close friend of Thomas Jefferson, was a war hero, and had been a senator from Virginia. He held several diplomatic positions in the Jefferson administration and was one of the diplomats who negotiated the Louisiana Purchase, almost doubling the size of the country. Under President Madison, Monroe was secretary of state. For their vice-presidential candidate, the Democratic-Republicans selected Daniel D. Tompkins of New York. Tompkins had been New York's governor.

The **Federalists**, now a party with little support outside the New England states, nominated Rufus King, their 1808 vice-presi-

▲ Monroe was the last of the "Virginia Dynasty"—Presidents Washington, Jefferson, Madison, and Monroe.

> "... few men were his equals in wisdom, firmness, and devotion to the country."
> —*John C. Calhoun, 1831*

Elizabeth Monroe (1768–1830) married James Monroe in 1786, although her well-to-do New York family did not approve of either his social status or politics. After their marriage, Elizabeth spent much of her time in Paris, where first her husband was ambassador to France and then to other countries. Elizabeth Monroe brought European formality to the White House when she became First Lady. Washington society thought she was too aristocratic and sometimes avoided her social receptions. Elizabeth was not fond of many of her duties as First Lady. After leaving the White House, the Monroes moved back to Oak Hill, their estate in Virginia. Elizabeth died and was buried there in 1830.

dential candidate, for the executive office. For the second spot, they chose John E. Howard of Maryland. Howard had been a soldier in the Revolution, a delegate to the Continental Congress, and a United States senator.

The Issues Now that the nation was again at peace, political issues did not divide the country. Throughout much of the country, the Federalists were disgraced for supporting the Hartford Convention in December 1814. At this meeting, held just before the end of the War of 1812, some extreme Federalists called for the New England states to **secede**, or leave the Union. Finally, the convention called for a series of Constitutional amendments that would weaken the

Federalist delegates from three New England states—Massachusetts, Connecticut, and Rhode Island—attended the Hartford Convention in December 1814. Because they opposed the War of 1812, some radical Federalists wanted to leave the Union. But moderate Federalists took control of the convention. They proposed five new constitutional amendments to reduce the power of the national government. These amendments would limit the president to one term, prevent Congress from passing a trade embargo for more than 60 days, keep naturalized citizens from serving in Congress, make it more difficult for new states to enter the Union, and require a two-thirds majority vote of Congress to declare war.

In January 1815, the Federalist delegates came to Washington, D.C., to discuss their proposals with President Madison and to force Congress to accept them. The unlucky men arrived in the capital as the city was celebrating General Andrew Jackson's stunning victory at the Battle of New Orleans. A few days later, word reached Washington that the Treaty of Ghent had been signed. The was was over! Great bonfires, loud parades, and fireworks celebrated the peace. A sense of patriotism swept the country, and many people believed the Federalists were traitors. The already unpopular Federalists lost even more support. The Federalists did not campaign in the presidential election of 1816, and by 1820, they had disappeared from the political scene.

government. However, the news of the convention reached Washington, D.C., just as the nation was celebrating Andrew Jackson's military victory over the British in New Orleans.

The demands of the Federalists were seen as an attack on the Union and the party was disgraced.

The Campaign Because political issues did not stir the country, virtually no campaigning went on. The Democratic-Republicans praised Monroe as a Revolutionary War hero and diplomat. The few supporters of the Federalist party did not campaign.

The Election Because Monroe and Tompkins carried every state except Massachusetts, Connecticut, and Delaware, they won 183 **electoral votes**. King and Howard won 34 electoral votes. The election of 1816 was the last in which the Federalist party nominated candidates for president and vice president. *See also* ELECTION OF 1804 (JEFFERSON); ELECTION OF 1808 (MADISON); ELECTION OF 1820 (MONROE).

Election of 1820

☿ James Monroe was unopposed for reelection. The Democratic-Republicans were the only national political party in the country.

The Candidates With James Monroe at the height of popularity and the nation at peace, the **Democratic-Republicans** easily renominated him. For vice president they again chose Daniel D. Tompkins. The weakened **Federalists** did not nominate any candidates.

The Issues The Monroe administration is sometimes called the "Era of Good Feelings" because it was a time of great **nationalism**, of peace, and of building within the nation. Yet this phrase is misleading,

▲ Monroe's administration enjoyed support from across the country.

- "The Era of Good Feelings"
—The Columbian Centinel, a Boston newspaper, describing Monroe's presidency

because two issues tore at the nation. The financial panic of 1819 caused an economic **depression**, or slowdown. Many banks and stores went out of business. In addition, the debate over the

Daniel D. Tompkins (1774–1825) wanted the presidency in 1816, but because he was not well known outside his home state, New York, he accepted the vice-presidential slot. He had served as a member of the United States House of Representatives, as a justice on the New York Supreme Court, and as governor of New York. Tompkins worked to abolish slavery in New York, for prison reform, and for better treatment of Native Americans. But he spent much of his time as vice president trying to clear his name in a financial scandal. After his death in 1825, investigators discovered that New York actually owed Tompkins about $92,000.

During his second term, President Monroe issued a policy that has influenced our country to the present day. In the early 1800s, Spain's Latin American colonies had revolted against Spanish rule and become independent nations. In addition, Russia, which already claimed Alaska, threatened to extend its empire south into the Oregon Country. Worried about Russian expansion and concerned that Spain would try to regain its former colonies, in 1823 Monroe issued a policy statement, later known as the Monroe Doctrine. He warned that the Americas were "henceforth not to be considered as subjects for future colonization by any European powers." Monroe's action was bold because the young United States was not strong enough to back up the new policy if it were challenged. Fortunately, Great Britain—then the most powerful nation on earth—agreed with America's spread of slavery grew. Congress argued over whether slavery should be extended into the new western territories. In 1819, when the Union had 22 states, 11 free and 11 slave, Missouri applied for admission as a slave state. A new slave state would upset the balance of representation in the Senate, where each state has two senators. In March 1820, President Monroe signed the Missouri Compromise. This law allowed Missouri to enter the Union as a slave state and Maine, which had been part of Massachusetts, as a free state. Thus representation in the Senate remained equal between North and South. The Compromise also stated that slavery would be "forever prohibited" in land north of the 36° 30′ line of latitude.

The Campaign President Monroe, as head of the nation's only political party, took no part in the debate over slavery nor was he blamed for the economic downturn. Monroe was at the peak of his popularity. With no opposing candidates, there was no campaign.

The Election Monroe and Tompkins received all the **electoral votes**—231—except one. One elector, William Plumer of New Hampshire, cast his vote for John Quincy Adams, Monroe's secretary of state and son of the second president. Plumer said he voted for Adams so that George Washington would remain the only president elected by a unanimous vote. *See also* ELECTION OF 1816 (MONROE).

Election of 1824

John Quincy Adams ✪ Adams's election was surrounded by conflict and controversy. He was accused of making a "corrupt bargain" to win office.

The Candidates By 1824, the **Democratic-Republicans** remained unchallenged, but they were seriously divided as a party. A party **caucus** was called, but only 66 of 261 congressional leaders attended. The caucus nominated William H. Crawford of Georgia for president. Other party members ignored this choice, because Crawford was paralyzed from a stroke. Albert Gallatin was chosen to run as vice president.

Shocked at the caucus's selection of Crawford, political leaders in Massachusetts declared John Quincy Adams, President Monroe's secretary of state and the son of John Adams, the second president, as their choice. Henry Clay, the powerful speaker of the House of Representatives, was chosen by the Kentucky legislature. As their candidate, the Tennessee legislature named Andrew Jackson, a senator and the hero of the Battle of New Orleans. John C. Calhoun of South Carolina became the nominee from his state. Because powerful congressional leaders—not the voters—controlled the caucus system, it was looked upon as undemocratic. This was the last election in which a caucus nominated candidates.

As the election heated up, Albert Gallatin took himself out of the vice presidential race. Calhoun, the youngest of the candidates, emerged as the vice-presidential nominee.

The Issues New political issues—**tariffs**, inter-

▲ Candidate Adams received most of his support from the New England states.

> • **"The people have been cheated."**
> —Andrew Jackson, after John Quincy Adams was declared president

nal improvements, such as roads and canals, and cheap public land—arose in the election. New England favored tariffs to protect its industries but opposed internal improvements and cheap land. The middle states also wanted high tariffs as well as internal improvements to open markets in the states west of the Appalachian Mountains. The agricultural South opposed tariffs, because they raised the costs of imported goods, and it also opposed most internal improvements. The South did favor cheap land, however. For the most part, each candidate represented the issues favored by his section of the country.

The Campaign In contrast to previous campaigns, this one was spirited and conflict-ridden. As before, the candidates did not travel or make speeches. Instead, newspaper articles and editorials throughout the nation took a central role praising or criticizing the candidates. In their sermons, ministers endorsed one presidential nominee and disapproved of the other. Henry Clay complained that "every liar . . . in the country was at work day and night to destroy my character." Exaggeration and **mudslinging** had reached new heights.

The Election When the **electoral votes** were counted, Jackson won 99, Adams 84, Crawford

41, and Clay 37. But Jackson's total was only a **plurality**, the most votes but not more than half. No one had won a **majority** of the electoral vote. Calhoun had clearly won the vice presidency, but the presidential contest was undecided.

Under the Constitution, the House of Representatives chose among the top three contenders. Because Clay came in fourth, he was out of the running, but he held great power in determining the final outcome. By asking his electors to support one of the other three candidates, he could in effect pick the president. Thus, supporters of Adams, Jackson, and Crawford all tried to sway Clay. But Clay had no trouble making his decision. He easily ruled out Crawford because of his poor health. Clay viewed Jackson as having little government experience, and Jackson also had competed with Clay for support in the western states. Clay chose Adams, whose political views were close to his own.

However, before openly supporting Adams, Clay called a confidential meeting between the two. To this day, no one knows the details of this meeting.

On February 9, 1825, the House met to make its choice, with each state having one vote. Of the 24 states in the Union, Adams won 13, Jackson 7, and Crawford 4. After Adams made Clay secretary of state, Jackson felt cheated, and his followers declared that a "corrupt bargain" had made Adams president. Although there remains no proof, they charged that Adams agreed to give Clay a Cabinet post in return for Clay's votes.

Furthermore, Jackson argued that the will of the people had been ignored and claimed Adams was guilty of fraud and corruption. He rallied his supporters to immediately begin the next presidential contest. In preparation, Jackson resigned his Senate seat and returned to Tennessee. *See also* ELECTION OF 1800 (JEFFERSON); ELECTION OF 1820 (MONROE); ELECTION OF 1828 (JACKSON).

Election of 1824

Candidate (Party)	Popular Vote	Electoral Vote
John Quincy Adams (Democratic-Republican)	113,122	84
Andrew Jackson (Democratic-Republican)	151,271	99
William Crawford (Democratic-Republican)	40,856	41
Henry Clay (Democratic-Republican)	47,531	37

Election **of 1828**

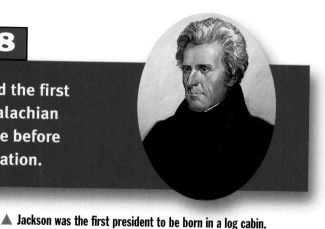

The Candidates Andrew Jackson and his supporters felt cheated by the 1824 election results (which had elected John Quincy Adams), and they immediately began the 1828 campaign, rallying around Jackson. Jackson's followers became known as **Democrats** and formed a new, well-organized political party. Adams's supporters became known as **National Republicans** and called for Adams's reelection. Thus, two political parties again competed in national elections.

John C. Calhoun, Adams's vice president, who now supported Jackson, became the Democratic choice for vice president. Richard Rush, who had been secretary of state in the Monroe administration (1817–1825), was selected for the number two spot on Adams's National Republican ticket.

The Issues Three main issues confronted the voters—the **tariff**, internal improvements, and **states' rights**. Again the nation was divided by region. The New England states, New York, and Pennsylvania favored a

▲ Jackson was the first president to be born in a log cabin.

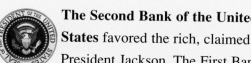

● "The people's candidate"
—*Democratic campaign slogan, 1828*

high tariff because it helped protect their manufacturers. The West also wanted the tariff but also favored internal improvements, which the Northeast did not. In general, the South opposed both the tariff and internal improvements. The South also favored states' rights, claiming that state governments were superior to the federal government. The North and the West usually opposed states' rights in favor of a strong central government.

The Second Bank of the United States favored the rich, claimed President Jackson. The First Bank of the United States had been established in George Washington's administration, but its charter expired in 1811. It was renewed for a 20-year term in 1816. During Jackson's first term, he vowed to destroy it. Jackson was successful when the bank became a campaign issue in the election of 1832. After Congress rechartered the bank, Jackson vetoed the bill. In his veto message, Jackson convincingly declared the bank an enemy of the people. His stand against the bank made him more popular than ever.

The Campaign Jackson's supporters attacked Adams from the beginning of his term in 1825. Adams had asked Congress to establish a national university and an astronomical observatory, and to build more roads and canals. The Jacksonians in Congress prevented most of Adams's plans from becoming law. Without the support of Congress, the Adams administration was not very successful. Adams himself was frustrated by the lack of progress.

Jackson's followers and managers started new campaign tactics. They organized rallies where Jackson's military victories, especially his triumph over the British at the Battle of New Orleans in 1815, were praised. They supplied newspapers with favorable stories about their candidate. A central committee in Washington, D.C., compiled lists of voters and sent them campaign material. The Jacksonians reminded voters that Adams "stole the presidency" in 1824 and that he had made a corrupt deal with Henry Clay, who had become Adams's secretary of state.

In return, Adams's followers struck back at Jackson. Newspapers that favored Adams called Jackson a gambler, a murderer, a thief, and a liar. They claimed Jackson was uneducated and, because of his military background, thirsted for blood. Jackson's marriage also became an issue. His enemies alleged that he had married his wife, Rachel, before she was divorced.

The campaign raged on with charges and countercharges. The National Republicans circulated the Coffin Handbill, a **broadside**, or small poster, with caskets printed on it. This handbill reminded voters that Jackson had approved the execution of six men who were tried and convicted of robbery, arson, and mutiny. In turn Adams was charged with being anti-Catholic. He was called a monarchist and was denounced for traveling on Sunday.

The parties actively looked for support in the German and Irish immigrant communities. For the first time, campaign literature from both sides was printed in German, as well as English.

The Election When the **electoral votes** were counted, Jackson won an overwhelming victory—178 electoral votes to Adams's 83. Because new, more democratic voting laws permitted a larger number of men to vote, and because voters were genuinely interested in the election outcome, the **popular vote** was three times as large as in 1824. Jackson was truly the people's candidate. *See also* ELECTION OF 1824 (JOHN QUINCY ADAMS); ELECTION OF 1832 (JACKSON).

Election of 1832

Andrew Jackson ✪ Jackson remained popular throughout his first term as president. He easily won reelection in 1832.

The Candidates The election of 1832 was the first in which political **conventions** were used to nominate candidates. Attended by delegates elected by the people, conventions were much more democratic than the **caucus** system. The first convention was held by the Anti-Mason party, the first **third party** in the United States. This party had been formed in 1827 to prevent Masons, members of a secret society, from holding office. For their candidate, they nominated William Wirt, a well-known speaker of the day.

At their convention, the **National Republicans** nominated Henry Clay, John Quincy Adams's secretary of state. For vice president, they chose John Sergeant, a Pennsylvania Congressman.

The **Democratic** convention easily nominated the popular Andrew Jackson. Vice President Calhoun, however, had resigned to become a South Carolina senator and work against Jackson's policies. For vice president, the Democrats named Martin Van Buren of New York. Van Buren was a long-time Jacksonian and had been Jackson's secretary of state.

The Issues The main issue in the election of 1832 was the rechartering of the Second Bank

▲ Jackson used his power to crush the Second Bank of the United States.

> "Shall the rights of the common man be respected or shall the rich rule the country again?"
>
> —*President Jackson, in his veto of the bank bill, 1832*

of the United States. Although the bank's charter did not expire until 1836, Henry Clay and his supporters convinced the bank's president, Nicholas Biddle, to ask Congress to renew the bank's charter in 1832. Clay assumed that if Jackson signed the bill, Jackson would lose support in the West and South, which opposed the bank. If he vetoed the bill, Jackson would lose support in the North, which generally favored the bank. In this way, Clay's chances for election in 1836 would be greatly improved.

After Congress passed the bank bill in July 1832, Jackson promptly vetoed it. In his veto message, he called the bank undemocratic, un-American, and unconstitutional. He stirred the support of the people by claiming the bank would "make the rich richer and the potent more powerful."

The Campaign As president, Jackson himself campaigned little, but his followers used the same tactics as they had in 1828. Because Jackson had so clearly identified the Bank of the United States as an enemy of the common people, Clay and the National Republicans found themselves with little support.

The Election Jackson again won a great victory—219 **electoral votes** to Clay's 49. Anti-Mason William Wirt received Vermont's 7 electoral votes. Jackson's victory made the Democrats the majority party. As a result of the election of 1832, the National Republicans came to an end and a new **political party**, the **Whigs**, was organized. The Whigs elected only two candidates to the presidency—William Henry Harrison (1841) and Zachary Taylor (1849–1850), only to have both men die in office. *See also* ELECTION OF 1828 (JACKSON); ELECTION OF 1836 (VAN BUREN); ELECTION OF 1840 (WILLIAM HENRY HARRISON); ELECTION OF 1848 (TAYLOR).

John C. Calhoun (1782–1850) was born into a wealthy South Carolina planter family. He was elected to Congress in 1811 and soon supported the War of 1812, becoming a leading War Hawk. In 1817, President Monroe appointed Calhoun secretary of war. Calhoun wanted the presidency in 1824, but with less support than either Adams or Jackson, he settled for the number two spot, becoming Adams's vice president. But Calhoun and Adams had very different political views. He quickly found that he opposed most of Adams's policies and worked to defeat them. In 1828 he became Andrew Jackson's running mate. But by about 1830, Vice President Calhoun had increasingly become a supporter of states' rights and was at odds with President Jackson. Two months before his term ended, he resigned the vice presidency to accept an appointment to a Senate seat from South Carolina.

Election of 1832

States (Total Number of Electoral Votes)	Andrew Jackson (Democrat)	Henry Clay (National Republican)
Alabama (7)	7	
Connecticut (8)		8
Delaware (3)		3
Georgia (11)	11	
Illinois (5)	5	
Indiana (9)	9	
Kentucky (15)		15
Louisiana (5)	5	
Maine (10)	10	
Maryland (10) *	3	5
Massachusetts (14)		14
Mississippi (4)	4	
Missouri (4)	4	
New Hampshire (7)	7	
New Jersey (8)	8	
New York (42)	42	
North Carolina (15)	15	
Ohio (21)	21	
Pennsylvania (30)	30	
Rhode Island (4)		4
South Carolina (11)**		
Tennessee (15)	15	
Vermont (7)+		
Virginia (23)	23	
Total (288)	**219**	**49**

* Two Maryland electors did not vote.

** South Carolina electors were appointed by the state legislature and opposed Jackson's candidacy; they cast their votes for John Floyd, the governor of Virginia.

+ Vermont's electors cast their votes for William Wirt of the Anti-Mason party.

Jackson received the people's support throughout the country.

Election of 1836

▲ Van Buren, a longtime Jackson supporter, promised to continue Jackson's policies.

The Candidates The **Democrats** met in Baltimore and, with Andrew Jackson's insistence, nominated Vice President Martin Van Buren for the presidency. For vice president, the Democrats chose Richard M. Johnson, a congressman from Kentucky and another of Jackson's followers.

During the previous four years, opposition to Jackson and the Democrats had increased and a new **political party**—the **Whigs**—was organized. This party was made up of former **Federalists**, supporters of the **National Republicans**, and members of the Anti-Mason party. The Whigs could not agree on one nominee, so they ran several regional candidates and hoped to throw the election into the House of Representatives. William Henry Harrison, who had defeated the Shawnee in the Battle of Tippecanoe in 1811, was a favorite from the West. Massachusetts supported Senator Daniel Webster and Tennessee nominated Senator Hugh L. White, who had hoped Jackson would secure the Democratic presidential nomination for him rather than Van Buren. North Carolina backed Senator William P. Magnum. As they did for the presidency, the Whigs backed no one vice-presidential candidate. Two favorites were put forward—Francis Granger of New York and John Tyler of Virginia.

> ● "I . . . believe
> ● him not only
> ● deserving
> ● of *my*
> ● confidence
> ● but the
> ● confidence
> ● of the
> ● Nation . . ."
> ● —*President Andrew Jackson,*
> ● *1829*

The Issues The policies of Andrew Jackson were the main issues in the election. Van Buren promised to continue Jackson's plans and work against the Bank of the United States. The Whigs were vehemently opposed to Jackson's policies and vowed to undo the policies of the previous eight years.

The Campaign Van Buren and the Democrats reminded the voters of Jackson's popularity. They noted that Van Buren would continue Jackson's policies for the next four years. The Democrats labeled Webster an old Federalist and criticized White because he deserted Jackson for his own political ambitions. They cast Harrison as a failure, both in the War of 1812 and as governor of the Indiana Territory. The Democrats raised money, distributed campaign material, and hosted rallies, dinners, and barbeques to help Van Buren's cause.

The divided Whigs criticized Van Buren, claiming he was not very intelligent, was corrupt, and was a snob. They also called him a "dandy" who was overly concerned about fashion and his personal appearance. Whigs in Congress called him "the little magician" because of his ability to always land on the

Hannah Van Buren (1783–1819) died 17 years before Martin Van Buren was elected president. She was born in Kinderhook, New York, and spoke Dutch as a child. She married Martin Van Buren in 1807 and they had four children. Little is known about Hannah Van Buren, and she left no writing of her own. Historians believe that she was a religious woman with great concern for the needy. After the family moved to Albany in 1817, she contracted tuberculosis. She died in 1819 at age 35.

winning side of an issue.

In addition, all the candidates were asked to answer questions about their political beliefs. These questions centered on the federal government's budget surplus, the sale of federal lands, the improvement of waterways, and the rechartering of the national bank. The candidates' responses were printed in newspapers across the country.

The Election When the **electoral votes** were counted, Van Buren had won a clear **majority**—170. The Whig candidates divided

the remaining 124 electoral votes. In the vice-presidential race, Richard Johnson was one vote from a majority. Thus the Senate, for the first and only time, chose between the two candidates who had received the most votes—Johnson and Whig Francis Granger. Because Vice President Van Buren was still presiding over the Senate, he made sure the senators chose Johnson. *See also* ELECTION OF 1828 (JACKSON); ELECTION OF 1832 (JACKSON); ELECTION OF 1840 (WILLIAM HENRY HARRISON).

Election of 1836		
Candidate (Party)	*Popular Vote*	*Electoral Vote*
Martin Van Buren (Democrat)	764,176	170
William Henry Harrison (Whig)	550,816	73
Hugh L. White (Whig)	146,107	26
Daniel Webster (Whig)	42,201	14
William P. Magnum (Whig)	0	11

Election of 1840

William Henry Harrison ✪ At age 68, William Henry Harrison was the oldest presidential candidate up to that time. He gave the longest Inaugural Address, but served the shortest term—one month.

The Candidates After their defeat in 1836, the **Whigs** rallied around William Henry Harrison, and the Whig convention easily nominated him. For vice president, they chose John Tyler of Virginia. He had joined the Whigs because he opposed Jackson, even though he supported most **Democratic** views.

The Democrats renominated Martin Van Buren without opposition. For vice president, they again chose Richard Johnson.

The Issues The Whigs charged that Van Buren and the Democrats were responsible for the financial panic of 1837 and the economic **depression** that followed. The Whigs tried to run on Harrison's military record and keep silent about national issues. The Democrats defended Van Buren and claimed that Harrison was old and sick and controlled by Whig leaders.

The Campaign The Whigs expanded upon the campaign tactics

▲ Harrison was the first Whig president.

> ● "Tippecanoe
> ● and Tyler
> ● too!"
> ● —Whig Campaign slogan, 1840

Virginian **John Tyler** was a Democrat who joined the Whigs because he disagreed with Andrew Jackson. When the Whigs put him on their 1840 ticket, they assumed that he would have little role in the administration. But after Harrison's death in 1841 he assumed the presidency and the duties of the office. Called "His Accidency" by those who opposed him, he made it clear the he was "president," not "acting president." Tyler quickly ran into trouble with the Whig-controlled Congress. His vetoes so angered the Whigs that they expelled Tyler from the party. Tyler then turned to the Democrats for support. But his past criticism of Andrew Jackson hurt his appeal. He was in effect a president without a party. *See also* ELECTION OF 1844.

used by the Democrats in previous elections. They portrayed Harrison as a man who preferred life in a log cabin rather than the White House. In reality, Harrison came from a well-to-do Virginia family, and had never lived in a log cabin. But the log cabin quickly became a symbol of Harrison's campaign. The Whigs held rallies, dinners, barbeques, and parades for the candidates.

The length of these events grew ever longer—two hours, then three, then five. Speeches, cheers, songs, and hard cider were part of every Whig gathering. "It is the ball a-rolling for Tippecanoe and Tyler too," sang the Whigs as they rolled a huge ball through the city streets. Thus the phrase "Keep the ball rolling" came into our language.

The Democrats tried the same tactics, but their efforts paled in comparison. The

Anna Harrison (1775–1864) was born in New Jersey but moved to Ohio with her family when she was about 20. In 1795 she met William Henry Harrison, a military officer, and the two eloped later that year. As an officer's wife she traveled with her husband until her family became too large. The Harrisons had ten children. Anna was better educated than most frontier women, as she had attended girls' schools in New Jersey. Anna was too ill to accompany president-elect Harrison when he left Ohio to go to Washington, D.C., in February 1841. She planned to wait for spring. But Harrison died after one month in office, and Anna never left Ohio.

Democrats said, "We urge the reelection of Van Buren because of his honesty, sagacity [wisdom], statesmanship . . . and the Whigs answer that Harrison is a poor man and lives in a log cabin." Above all, the Whigs were determined to win.

The Election Harrison and Tyler carried the election with 234 **electoral votes** to Van Buren's and Johnson's 60. Harrison took the oath of office outside on a rainy, cold, and windy March 4. His rambling Inaugural Address lasted for about one hour and 45 minutes. He caught a cold, which developed into pneumonia, and he died on April 4, 1841. John Tyler became the first vice president to succeed a president who had died in office. *See also* ELECTION OF 1828 (JACKSON); ELECTION OF 1832 (JACKSON); ELECTION OF 1836 (VAN BUREN).

Election of 1840

States (Total Number of Electoral Votes)	Martin Van Buren (Democrat)	William Henry Harrison (Whig)
Alabama (7)	7	
Arkansas (3)	3	
Connecticut (8)		8
Delaware (3)		3
Georgia (11)		11
Illinois (5)	5	
Indiana (9)		9
Kentucky (15)		15
Louisiana (5)		5
Maine (10)		10
Maryland (10)		10
Massachusetts (14)		14
Michigan (3)		3
Mississippi (4)		4
Missouri (4)	4	
New Hampshire (7)	7	
New Jersey (8)		8
New York (42)		42
North Carolina (15)		15
Ohio (21)		21
Pennsylvania (30)		30
Rhode Island (4)		4
South Carolina (11)	11	
Tennessee (15)		15
Vermont (7)		7
Virginia (23)	23	
Total (294)	**60**	**234**

Harrison and the Whigs campaigned hard and won a sizeable victory in the Electoral College.

Election of 1844

James K. Polk ✪ Democrat James K. Polk was a surprise candidate for the presidency in 1844. He won a very close race.

The Candidates Many **Democrats** believed they should nominate former president Van Buren to run again in 1844. But southern Democrats opposed Van Buren because he was against the **annexation** of Texas and westward expansion. They preferred Lewis Cass of Michigan, who favored westward expansion. The convention became **deadlocked**, with neither of the favorites able to win the nomination. A delegate then suggested James K. Polk, a former Tennessee governor and a follower of Andrew Jackson, for the nomination. Polk thus became the first **dark-horse** candidate nominated by a major party. For vice president, the Democrats chose George M. Dallas of Pennsylvania. Dallas had recently served as Van Buren's minister to Russia.

Because the **Whigs** had kicked Tyler out of the party, they turned to well-known party leader Henry Clay. At

▲ Polk's campaign promised to expand the borders of the United States.

> "Fifty-four Forty or Fight!"
> —Democratic campaign slogan, 1844

Sarah Polk (1803–1891) was born on her father's plantation in Tennessee. She attended a private school in Nashville and then spent one year at a female academy in North Carolina. She met James Polk in 1819 and they married in 1824. A well-educated and politically minded woman, Sarah Polk played a key role in her husband's career. She encouraged his political goals and activities. After becoming First Lady, she worked with her husband on political matters and as his private secretary. A devout Presbyterian, Sarah Polk banned drinking and dancing at the White House, much to Washington society's shock. After leaving the White House in 1849, the Polks returned to their home in Nashville. James Polk died three months later, but Sarah lived at their home until 1891.

the Whig convention, he was nominated by **acclamation**. For vice president, the Whigs backed Theodore Frelinghuysen of New Jersey.

A new third party, the Abolitionists, nominated James G. Birney. This **political party** favored **abolition**, an immediate end to slavery in the United States.

The Issues The major issue facing the nation was the annexation of Texas. Until 1836 Texas had been a part of Mexico, but American settlers living there won independence that year. The Texans wanted to become part of the United States, but the majority in Congress refused to admit Texas. Northerners were concerned that slavery would spread into Texas. They also worried that annexation might start a war with Mexico. Southerners wanted to add not only Texas but the Mexican lands of California and New Mexico as well.

Another key issue was the Oregon Territory, which had been jointly occupied by the United States and Great Britain since 1818. Over the years many Americans had settled there. Some now wanted the United States to completely take over the entire area, up to the latitude line of 54° 40′.

The Campaign At the beginning of the campaign, it was clear that the Whigs and the Abolitionists were opposed to westward expansion, especially the annexation of Texas. But most Democrats favored Manifest Destiny, the idea that the United States was certain to reach to the Pacific Ocean.

To sway the voters, both parties reached new levels of **mudslinging** and fraud. The Democrats claimed Clay was a heavy drinker, a gambler, and a good-for-nothing. They also brought back the charges of the "corrupt bar-gain" from the ELECTION OF 1824. In turn, the Whigs said Polk was a petty scoundrel and a slave driver.

Democratic political **bosses** rushed the naturalization of immigrants so they could vote for Polk. In Louisiana, one boss sent a boat filled with Democrats up the Mississippi River. It then stopped at three different ports so the men could vote at each place.

The Election The **popular vote** was close— about 1,337,000 for the Democrats to 1,299,000 for the Whigs. Polk and Dallas received 170 **electoral votes**. Clay and Frelinghuysen won 105. If Clay had carried the 36 electoral votes of New York, the Whigs would have won the election. But abolitionist Birney polled about 62,300 votes in New York, thus taking votes away from Clay. The state's electoral votes went to Polk. *See also* ELECTION OF 1824 (JOHN QUINCY ADAMS); ELECTION OF 1828 (JACKSON); ELECTION OF 1832 (JACKSON); ELECTION OF 1836 (VAN BUREN); ELECTION OF 1840 (WILLIAM HENRY HARRISON).

Election of 1848

⚡ Zachary Taylor was the first president with no political experience before being elected. Most people did not even know what his political views were.

The Candidates Eager to win the White House, the **Whigs** passed over the well-known Henry Clay and instead nominated Zachary Taylor. Taylor had been a successful general in the Mexican-American War (1846–1848) but had no political experience. For vice president, the Whigs chose Millard Fillmore from New York.

President Polk, the **incumbent**, or a person already in office, decided not to run for reelection. The **Democrats** turned to Lewis Cass, who had also been a general in the Mexican-American War. William O. Butler was nominated for vice president. Butler had served in the War of 1812 and the Mexican-American War, as well as in Congress.

Some Democrats and others who opposed the extension of slavery, a group called the Free Soilers, left the convention and later nominated former president Martin Van Buren as their choice for the White House.

▲ Taylor, a Whig, served one year and four months of his term as president.

- • "Free Soil,
- • Free Speech,
- • Free Labor,
- • and Free
- • Men."
- •
- • —*Campaign slogan of the Free Soilers, who opposed Taylor*

Millard Fillmore (1800–1874) was elected as Zachary Taylor's vice president and became the thirteenth president after Taylor died suddenly in 1850. Fillmore, a New York lawyer, had a wealth of experience before becoming president, including serving in the United States House of Representatives. After Taylor's death, Fillmore worked to secure the Compromise of 1850, which calmed the slavery issue that was tearing at the country. He also oversaw the modernization of the White House, secured federal money for railroad construction, and sent Commodore Matthew Perry to open trade with Japan in early 1853. Still, Fillmore was passed over by the Whigs for the presidential nomination in 1852. In 1856, Fillmore was the presidential nominee of the Know-Nothing party. *See also* ELECTION OF 1852 (PIERCE); ELECTION OF 1856 (BUCHANAN).

The Issues Slavery was the main issue in the election and it divided both major parties. The Whigs, most of whom were from the North, had opposed the Mexican-American War and now wanted to keep slavery from spreading. Yet Taylor, their candidate, was from Louisiana and owned hundreds of slaves. Most Democrats, the majority party in the South, had supported the war. They believed that slavery should be allowed in the new lands. When these territories became states, they planned to allow slavery and thus keep an equal balance between free states and slave states in the Senate. Cass, from Michigan, did not own slaves, but he believed that slaveholders should be allowed to take their "property" with them as they moved west.

Election of 1848

States (Total Number of Electoral Votes)	Zachary Taylor (Whig)	Lewis Cass (Democrat)
Alabama (9)		9
Arkansas (3)		3
Connecticut (6)	6	
Delaware (3)	3	
Florida (3)	3	
Georgia (10)	10	
Illinois (9)		9
Indiana (12)		12
Iowa (4)		4
Kentucky (12)	12	
Louisiana (6)	6	
Maine (9)		9
Maryland (8)	8	
Massachusetts (12)	12	
Michigan (5)		5
Mississippi (6)		6
Missouri (7)		7
New Hampshire (6)		6
New Jersey (7)	7	
New York (36)	36	
North Carolina (11)	11	
Ohio (23)		23
Pennsylvania (26)	26	
Rhode Island (4)	4	
South Carolina (9)		9
Tennessee (13)	13	
Texas (4)		4
Vermont (6)	6	
Virginia (17)		17
Wisconsin (4)		4
Total (290)	**163**	**127**

Whig Zachary Taylor won a close race, partly because the Democrats and the Free Soil party split the popular vote in key states.

The Campaign The issue of slavery dominated the campaign. In general, northern Democrats and northern Whigs tried not to take a stand on the slavery issue. In this way they hoped to keep the support of northern voters. The southern branches of the parties favored the extension of slavery into the new lands recently acquired from Mexico. The Free Soilers, and other minor parties, directly opposed the growth of slavery.

The Election Because the Democratic vote was split between Cass and Van Buren, the Whigs won the election. Taylor and Fillmore won 163 **electoral votes**. Cass and Butler won 127. Although Van Buren did not receive any electoral votes, he received enough of the popular vote in New York to cause that state's 36 electoral votes to go to Taylor. This gave the Whigs the election. Taylor, however, died on July 9, 1850, and Millard Fillmore became president. *See also* ELECTION OF 1836 (VAN BUREN); ELECTION OF 1840 (WILLIAM HENRY HARRISON); ELECTION OF 1844 (POLK).

Election of 1852

✪ Just before the Civil War (1861–1865), the issue of slavery deeply divided the country. Pierce won as a "compromise candidate." He was from the North and had a campaign that pleased the South.

The Candidates The **Democratic** party nominated Franklin Pierce, a **dark-horse** candidate, when it could not decide among party favorites. Pierce, a former senator from New Hampshire, was little known outside his home state. The **Whigs** chose General Winfield Scott, who had earned fame in the Mexican-American War (1846–1848).

The Free Soilers nominated John Parker Hale of New Hampshire for president. As before, the Free Soilers remained a party with one issue—opposition to slavery.

The Issues Slavery threatened to tear the country apart. Pierce and the Democrats favored the Compromise of 1850. These laws tried to hold the Union together by preserving slavery in the South while enforcing a strict Fugitive Slave Law to return runaway slaves. The Whigs also supported the Compromise of 1850. This caused

> ● "We Polked
> ● you in 1844;
> ● we shall
> ● Pierce you
> ● in 1852!"
> ● —*Democratic party slogan, 1852*

▲ Democrat Pierce, at age 48, was the youngest president to have been elected up to that time.

many northern Whigs to leave and join the antislavery Free Soil Party.

The Campaign Pierce stayed home in New Hampshire and let others campaign for him. General Scott broke with tradition and actively campaigned—a first for a presidential candidate. He traveled to Kentucky, Ohio, Pennsylvania, and New York trying to overcome the Democrats' charges that he was against immigrants.

The Election Pierce won the election of 1852 by a majority—1,601,274 votes to Scott's 1,386,580. In the **Electoral College**, Pierce won a 250–to–42 victory. Pierce's election led to the end of the Whig party. *See also* ELECTION OF 1844 (POLK); ELECTION OF 1848 (TAYLOR).

Because the Pierces' first two sons died in childhood, their third son, Bennie, became the center of their lives. Two months before Franklin Pierce's inauguration, the family was traveling by train when their passenger car derailed and eleven-year-old Bennie was crushed to death before their eyes. Mrs. Pierce never recovered from the shock.

Jane Pierce (1806–1863) Jane Means Appleton married Congressman Franklin Pierce in 1834 and they moved to Washington, D.C. She hated politics and tried to convince her husband to quit. After learning of her husband's nomination for president in 1852, she prayed for his defeat. She did not appear in public as First Lady until 1855—almost two years after Pierce's inauguration.

Election of 1856

✪ The growing controversy over slavery threatened the nation as the election of 1856 approached. Buchanan and the Democrats offered little to resolve the issue.

The Candidates The **Democrats** were deeply divided over the issue of slavery. The North opposed two leading candidates for the nomination—President Franklin Pierce and Senator Stephen A. Douglas. Douglas had sponsored the Kansas-Nebraska Act, which permitted slavery to spread north, and Pierce had signed the bill into law. The Democrats then compromised by nominating James Buchanan of Pennsylvania. Buchanan had a great deal of experience, but because he had recently been minister to Great Britain, he was not involved in the slavery controversy.

A new, well-organized **political party** emerged in the North—the **Republican party**. At their convention, they nominated John C. Frémont, a hero of the Mexican-American War (1846-1848). William L. Dayton of New Jersey became their vice-presidential choice.

In the late 1850s, another political party, the American or "Know-Nothing" party, emerged. They were called the "Know-Nothings" because when asked about the party's beliefs, they responded "I know nothing." This group opposed foreigners and Roman Catholics and called for strict immigration laws to protect American workers. They nominated former president Millard Fillmore as their candidate. The remnants of the Whig party also supported Fillmore.

> ● "Free Speech,
> ● Free Press,
> ● Free Soil,
> ● Free Men,
> ● Frémont, and
> ● Victory"
> ●
> ● —1856 Republican
> ● campaign slogan

▲ Democrat Buchanan was the only president who never married.

The Issues The ongoing debate over slavery and its spread to the territories tore at the nation. In Kansas, fighting raged over whether the territory should be admitted to the Union as a free state or a slave state. The nation was becoming increasingly divided—North against South.

The Campaign The Republicans campaigned on a slogan of "Free Speech, Free Press, Free Soil, Free Men, Frémont, and Victory!" This slogan was carried on banners and shouted in torchlight processions and political rallies. Scientists, clergy, and teachers all spoke out for the Republicans—and against slavery. Writers Ralph Waldo Emerson and Henry Wadsworth Longfellow encouraged voters to support the Republican cause.

In addition to the typical **mudslinging** during the campaign, the Democrats added a threat—if Frémont won, the South would **secede**, and the Union would then break apart.

The Election Buchanan won 174 **electoral votes** to Frémont's 114 and Fillmore's 8 from Maryland. The nation was increasingly divided. Buchanan won all the southern states and some in the North. But Frémont's support was all in the North. *See also* ELECTION OF 1852 (PIERCE); ELECTION OF 1860 (LINCOLN).

Election of 1856

States (Total Number of Electoral Votes)	James Buchanan (Democrat)	John C. Frémont (Republican)
Alabama (9)	9	
Arkansas (4)	4	
California (4)	4	
Connecticut (6)		6
Delaware (3)	3	
Florida (3)	3	
Georgia (10)	10	
Illinois (11)	11	
Indiana (13)	13	
Iowa (4)		4
Kentucky (12)	12	
Louisiana (6)	6	
Maine (8)		8
Maryland (8) *		
Massachusetts (13)		13
Michigan (6)		6
Mississippi (7)	7	
Missouri (9)	9	
New Hampshire (5)		5
New Jersey (7)	7	
New York (35)		35
North Carolina (10)	10	
Ohio (23)		23
Pennsylvania (27)	27	
Rhode Island (4)		4
South Carolina (8)	8	
Tennessee (12)	12	
Texas (4)	4	
Vermont (5)		5
Virginia (15)	15	
Wisconsin (5)		5
Total (296)	**174**	**114**

* Maryland's eight electors cast their ballots for former President Millard Fillmore, running on the American, or Know-Nothing, party.

Support for the new Republican party was in the Northern states.

⁓⁓⁓⁓⁓⁓⁓⁓⁓⁓

John C. Breckinridge (1821–1875), a successful lawyer, was elected to the Kentucky legislature in 1849 and two years later to the United States House of Representatives. He was elected in 1856 as James Buchanan's vice president. Breckinridge believed the Union could be saved if slavery were allowed in the western territories. In 1860, the Southern Democrats nominated him for president. (He lost the presidency, but Kentucky had elected him to the Senate.) Breckinridge, along with several members of Congress, looked for a way to end the looming crisis of civil war. He supported the Crittenden Compromise. This plan would guarantee slavery where it already existed and extend the Missouri Compromise line to the Pacific Coast, allowing slavery south of the line. But Congress rejected this plan.

Breckinridge personally favored secession, but he stayed in the Senate. At first he supported Kentucky's attempt to remain neutral, but he believed his home state should leave the Union if attempts at compromise failed. As the crisis deepened, Breckinridge began attacking President Lincoln's policies. He opposed Lincoln's plan to raise an army to put down the rebellion. After Union forces took control of Kentucky, he openly supported the Confederacy. The federal government charged him with treason. He fought for the Confederacy and later served in the Confederate government. After the war, he fled to Cuba and then to Europe. In 1868, after President Andrew Johnson declared **amnesty**, or a pardon, for all who fought against the Union, Breckinridge returned to Kentucky, where he died in 1875. *See also* ELECTION OF 1860.

Election of 1860

✪ Lincoln had little national political experience before the 1860 campaign. Because of his party's stand on slavery, however, his nomination divided the nation as never before.

▲ Lincoln was the first Republican president.

The Candidates Several **Republicans** sought the 1860 Republican nomination. The leading candidates included Senator William Seward of New York, Edward Bates of Missouri, Governor Salmon P. Chase and Senator Benjamin Wade of Ohio, and Abraham Lincoln of Illinois. The Republicans held their convention in Chicago, Illinois, at a convention hall called the Wigwam, which had been built especially for them. On the third **ballot**, or round of voting, Lincoln won the nomination. For vice president, the Republicans chose Hannibal Hamlin of Maine.

The **Democrats** were divided between **factions** from the North and the South. They held their convention in Charleston, South Carolina, where the leading candidate was Stephen A. Douglas of Illinois. Trying to sway the convention, southern delegates demanded that the party's **platform** be voted on before the candidate was nominated. Two platforms were presented—one protecting slavery and one opposing it. After the convention approved the antislavery platform, most southern delegates walked out in protest. Balloting for the candidate began, but the convention **deadlocked**, and no agreement was reached. The Democrats agreed to meet again in Baltimore in June 1860.

> "In your hands, my dissatisfied countrymen, and not mine, is the momentous issue of civil war. . . ."
>
> —*Abraham Lincoln,*
> *First Inaugural Address,*
> *March 4, 1861*

In Baltimore the delegates again could not agree on a candidate. When Douglas gained some support, many angry southern delegates withdrew. The remaining delegates finally nominated Douglas and he became the candidate of the northern Democrats. For vice president, the northern Democrats chose Herschel V. Johnson of Georgia.

The southern delegates met again and nominated John C. Breckinridge of Kentucky for president and Joseph Lane of Oregon for vice president. The Democratic party was now split.

Meanwhile, another **political party**—the **Constitutional Union party**—was organized. This group nominated John Bell of Tennessee for president and Edward Everett, a former four-term Massachusetts governor, for vice president.

The Issues Slavery divided the nation. By 1860 most northerners opposed the spread of slavery into the territories. However, some northerners—**abolitionists**—called for the immediate end to slavery wherever it existed in the United States. In contrast, most southerners

The Election of 1860

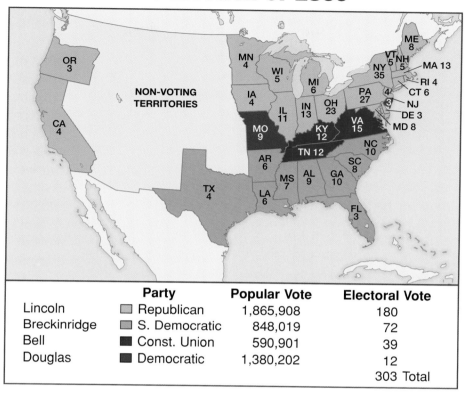

Party		Popular Vote	Electoral Vote
Lincoln	Republican	1,865,908	180
Breckinridge	S. Democratic	848,019	72
Bell	Const. Union	590,901	39
Douglas	Democratic	1,380,202	12
			303 Total

Four candidates won electoral votes in the election of 1860. Lincoln won in the northern states, Breckinridge in the southern states, and Bell and Douglas won in the border states.

demanded that slavery continue where it was established and that it be allowed to spread west. Even white southerners who did not hold slaves tended to support slavery. For many, slavery was a key part of southern life, and the South's agricultural economy depended on it. Southerners also noted that slavery was permitted under the Constitution, and they believed it was their right to hold slaves.

The Campaign Douglas quickly became the most active candidate in the campaign. He traveled throughout the country and urged the preservation of the Union. He stood behind his **popular-sovereignty** platform—the idea that the people in each territory could decide for themselves whether or not to allow slavery. Douglas campaigned in the North and in the South. He warned that a Lincoln victory would cause the South to secede from the Union.

Breckinridge remained in the South and did little campaigning himself. He defended slavery and asserted his love of the Constitution. Most southern leaders, clergy, and newspapers supported Breckinridge and defended the South's way of life.

Bell and the Constitutional Unionists, called "Bellringers," held parades and tried to rally the voters. Their one goal was to preserve the Union and to return to the ways of the past. Most of their support came from the border states in the middle of the country—Kentucky, Tennessee, and Virginia.

Lincoln himself did not campaign. He claimed that his views were already well known. His Republican supporters throughout the North, however, paraded, marched, and rallied to get out the vote. Torchlight parades, with banners and flags, lit up nighttime skies. A "rail-splitter's battalion" of men, each six feet, four inches tall—as tall as Lincoln in his stocking feet—marched through the streets of Boston. Because each candidate had strong support in different parts of the country, the outcome was in doubt until the very end.

The Election It was a sectional election. Lincoln received no votes in the South—he was not even on most southern state ballots. Breckinridge won no northern electoral votes. The election was close in many states. In New Jersey, the outcome was not known for days after the election. Lincoln carried California by a margin of only 657 popular votes out of more that 80,000 cast.

When the votes were finally counted, Lincoln had won with 180 **electoral votes** and 1,865,908 **popular**

Mary Todd Lincoln (1818–1882) was born to a well-to-do Kentucky family. She received a good education, spoke French, and studied dance and music. When she was 21, she moved to Springfield, Illinois, to live with her sister. There she met Abraham Lincoln, whom she married when she was 24.

Her personal life was troubled, and she was often depressed. The Lincolns' second son, Edward, died in 1850 at age 4; their third child, Willie, died in 1862 at age 11. Mary Lincoln was crushed by these losses. While First Lady, Mary was criticized because her brother and three half-brothers fought for the South. Her White House receptions were called inappropriate during the dark times of the Civil War.

After Lincoln's assassination in 1865, Mary did not attend the funeral; she spent five weeks in mourning in the White House. After returning to Springfield, her actions grew even more strange. She believed she was deeply in debt but spent money frivolously on dresses, hats, and jewelry. After her youngest son, Tad, died in 1871, Mary became more disturbed. Her oldest and only surviving son, Robert, committed her to a mental hospital. She was released after three months and went to live with her sister in Springfield, where she died a sick and unhappy woman in 1882.

votes. Douglas earned 1,380,202 popular votes, but carried only the 9 votes of Missouri and 3 of New Jersey's 7 votes, for a total of 12 electoral votes. Breckinridge carried the South—72 electoral votes and 848,019 popular votes. Bell won 39 electoral votes and 590,901 popular votes.

Lincoln promised to prevent slavery from extending west and to limit it to only where it now existed. This threatened the South. On December 20, 1860, South Carolina called a convention to consider secession from the Union. The convention declared that South Carolina had decided to leave the Union. Other southern states soon followed suit. Before Lincoln was inaugurated on March 4, 1861, seven states seceded. Four additional states later joined them. President Buchanan took no action, saying the president could not decide the relations between the states and the federal government. *See also* ELECTION OF 1856 (BUCHANAN); ELECTION OF 1864 (LINCOLN).

Election of 1864

Abraham Lincoln ☉ While the Civil War raged in 1864, the nation voted for president. Lincoln remained committed to the Union cause, but others called for peace at any cost.

The Candidates When the Civil War erupted on April 12, 1861, both sides expected a short conflict. It soon became clear that the war would drag on, as neither side could score a decisive victory. As the 1864 election approached, Lincoln was blamed for the North's failures. Some **Republicans** wanted to choose another candidate—Secretary of the Treasury Salmon P. Chase—but Lincoln had enough support to win the nomination. For vice president, they chose **Democrat** Andrew Johnson, the only southern senator who remained loyal to the Union. By calling themselves National Unionists, the Republicans hoped to appeal to loyal northern Democrats.

Many northern Democrats were opposed to the war. They noted that the war had lasted four years with no end in sight. These "Copperheads"—Democrats who opposed the war—chose former Union general George McClellan for president and George H. Pendleton, a representative from Ohio, for vice president. Pendleton was one of the leaders of the Copperheads.

The Issues The outcome of the Civil War was *the* issue of the election. Lincoln, the Republicans, and loyal Democrats supported the Union and the defeat of the Confederacy. Lincoln had already increased support for the

> • "With malice
> • toward none,
> • with charity
> • for all . . ."
> —Abraham Lincoln,
> Second Inaugural Address,
> March 4, 1865

▲ Lincoln did not believe he would be reelected.

war among **abolitionists** by issuing the Emancipation Proclamation, which declared that all enslaved people living in the Confederacy were freed. The Proclamation, which became effective on January 1, 1863, broadened the war's goal to include ending slavery, as well as saving the Union.

In an attempt to gain the voters' support, the Democrats called for an immediate cease-fire. They also promised to negotiate with the South to restore the Union.

The Campaign Although McClellan had accepted the Democratic nomination, he refused to run on their platform. He noted that he could not "face my gallant comrades of the army and navy . . . and tell them that their labors and sacrifices have been in vain." He stressed that "No peace can be permanent without Union." But Democratic party leaders, trying to sway the voters, attacked Lincoln as incompetent, corrupt, and unable to win the war.

At first, the campaign looked bleak for the Republicans, as the South continued to avoid defeat. But, after the Union victories at Atlanta and Mobile Bay, the tide turned. As news of

Andrew Johnson (1808–1875), born on the North Carolina frontier, received no formal education. At age 13, he was apprenticed to a tailor, and his fellow workers taught him the basics of reading and writing. Around 1826, he convinced his parents to move west with him, and they settled in Greeneville, Tennessee. There he met Eliza McCardle, whom he married the following year. She continued to improve his education. In 1828, he became mayor of Greeneville and was then elected as a Democrat to the Tennessee legislature. By 1843, he was serving in the United States Congress.

After Abraham Lincoln won the presidency in 1860, Johnson was the only southern senator to remain loyal to the United States. After Union forces captured Tennessee, Lincoln appointed Johnson as military governor. With Johnson's urging, Tennessee became the only southern state to outlaw slavery before the 1863 Emancipation Proclamation. As the election of 1864 approached, Lincoln and the Republicans (renamed the National Unionists) tried to appeal to loyal Democrats, and they selected Johnson, a Democrat, as vice president. He had served as vice president for only six weeks when Lincoln was assassinated.

The burden of rebuilding the war-torn nation thus fell to Johnson. He quickly ran into conflict with the Radical Republicans who controlled Congress. In 1868 he became the first president to be **impeached**, but the Senate acquitted him by one vote. After completing his term in 1869, he returned to Tennessee. Later in 1874, he was again elected to the United States Senate. He had served five months of his term when he the Union's success spread, the Republicans grew confident of victory. Even former Treasury secretary Chase campaigned for Lincoln. Soon most northern newspapers supported Lincoln as well.

The Election Lincoln won a decisive victory—121 **electoral votes** to McClellan's 12. In the **popular vote**, Lincoln earned 2,218,388 votes as compared to the Democrats' 1,812,807. The troops overwhelmingly supported Lincoln. Their ballots were counted separately—Lincoln scored about 117,000 votes to McClellan's 34,000. Lincoln carried every state except Kentucky, New Jersey, and Delaware. The states of the Confederacy did not vote. *See* ELECTION OF 1860.

When Lincoln's second term began on March 4, 1865, it appeared that the Civil War would soon end. On April 9, Confederate General Robert E. Lee surrendered to General Ulysses S. Grant, the commander of the Union forces. Five days later, Lincoln was shot by John Wilkes Booth, a Confederate sympathizer. Lincoln died early on the morning of April 15, and Andrew Johnson was sworn in as president. *See also* ELECTION OF 1860 (LINCOLN); ELECTION OF 1868 (GRANT).

Election of 1868

The Candidates The **Republican** nominating convention in Chicago had no difficulty selecting a presidential nominee. Ulysses S. Grant, the man who saved the Union by winning the Civil War, was an ideal candidate. Grant was well known, popular, likeable, and because he had no political experience, he had a clean record. The convention nominated him by **acclamation**—wild shouts and cheers. The second spot on the **ticket** was hotly contested. Among those who sought the vice presidency were Senator Benjamin Wade of Ohio, Senator Henry Wilson of Massachusetts, New York governor Reuben E. Fenton, and Speaker of the House Schuyler Colfax. Finally Colfax was chosen on the fifth **ballot**.

Several **Democratic** leaders wanted their party's nomination. The favorites were Chief Justice Salmon P. Chase, George Pendleton of Ohio, Senator Thomas

▲ Grant was a Civil War hero with no political experience.

> ● **"Let us have peace."**
> ●
> ● —*Ulysses S. Grant, nomination acceptance letter, 1868*

The phrase "Waving the bloody shirt" stems from the 1868 campaign. One night in March 1868, a northern tax collector in Mississippi was whipped, receiving 75 lashes by members of the Ku Klux Klan. This terrorist group, dedicated to white supremacy, then threatened to kill him if he did not leave the state in ten days. The tax collector reported this incident to the military authorities. An army officer took the bloodstained shirt and gave it to Benjamin Butler, a Radical Republican congressman from Massachusetts. A few days later, Butler proposed a bill that would allow the president to send the army to enforce federal laws in the South. As he spoke he waved the shirt. From that time on, many Republican speakers "waved the bloody shirt" as they blamed the South for starting the Civil War.

Hendricks of Indiana, Civil War hero General Winfield Scott, and Francis P. Blair of Missouri. Even President Andrew Johnson had some support. When the convention became deadlocked, Horatio Seymour, a former New York governor and a peace Democrat who opposed the Civil War, was offered as a **compromise candidate**. Seymour had not sought the nomination but won it on the twenty-second ballot. For vice president the Democrats chose Francis P. Blair, Jr., who had been a general in the Civil War.

The Issues The reconstruction of the South was the central issue of the campaign. During the Johnson administration, the Radical Republicans had imposed strict laws on the defeated states. In general, these laws were designed to protect the newly freed

African Americans and to keep those who rebelled against the Union out of government. Most southerners and some northerners believed these policies were too harsh and hoped to bring the southern states back into the Union quickly to help heal the wounds of the war.

Another war-related issue focused on the nation's currency. During the war, investors, mostly from the East, bought federal Civil War bonds with greenbacks, or paper money. Because these greenbacks had little value, investors wanted to be paid in gold. Many people, especially those in the West, demanded the investors be paid in greenbacks.

The Campaign The 1868 campaign was filled with **mudslinging** and slander. The Democratic newspapers charged that Grant was a thief who stole silver during the Civil War. They claimed he was a drunk and that he was anti-Semitic. In turn, the Republicans claimed that Seymour had called New York draft rioters "my friends," thus questioning his loyalty to the Union. They said insanity ran in his family and therefore Seymour, too, must be insane.

Both parties made strong efforts to win in the South. As the former Confederate states rejoined the Union, the parties worked to register African Americans to vote—many for the first time. Because President Lincoln was a Republican, most African Americans supported the Republican party. During the Civil War, he had issued the Emancipation Proclamation, which declared enslaved African

The Republican party was sure of victory in the 1868 presidential election.

Americans in the rebellious states to be free.

The Election Grant won the election with 214 **electoral votes** to Seymour's 80. The Republicans earned 3,013,650 popular votes to the Democrats' 2,708,744. But if Grant had not won the votes of about one-half million recently freed African Americans, he would have probably lost the election. Of the former Confederate states, Grant carried North Carolina, South Carolina, Florida, Alabama, and Tennessee. Seymour won only Georgia and Louisiana. Texas, Virginia, and Mississippi had not yet been readmitted to the Union and thus were not able to vote. *See also* ELECTION OF 1864 (LINCOLN); ELECTION OF 1872 (GRANT).

Election of 1872

Ulysses S. Grant ✪ Corruption in Grant's first administration caused the Republican party to split in two. Yet Grant still won an overwhelming victory in 1872.

The Candidates President Grant was not a good judge of character, and he often surrounded himself with corrupt and dishonest men. As the people around Grant schemed and made money through **graft**—illegal means—and corruption, some **Republicans** called for **reform**, or changes. When reforms were defeated, these **Liberal** Republicans called their own convention in early 1872 to nominate someone other than Grant for president. One of the leading Liberal Republican candidates was Charles Francis Adams, the grandson of President John Adams and the son of President John Quincy Adams. Another was Lyman Trumbull, a former senator. But after the fifth **ballot**, the leading contenders could not win a majority of the convention votes. On the sixth ballot, the Liberal Republicans nominated Horace Greeley, the editor of the New York *Tribune*. Greeley had long called for reform and honest government but was hardly a political leader. Many reformers were shocked by the choice. For vice president, the Liberal Republicans selected Benjamin Gratz Brown, a reform-minded governor of Missouri.

The regular Republicans stood behind President Grant and nominated him by **acclamation**. For vice president, the Republicans chose Henry Wilson of Massachusetts.

The **Democrats** were in disarray and desperately wanted to remove President Grant. Rather than choose their own candidate, they decided

▲ An honest man, Grant was not involved in the scandals of his presidency.

> "Grant us another term."
>
> —Republican campaign slogan, 1872

to support Greeley and Gratz Brown. Those Democrats who did not support Greeley held a separate convention and nominated Charles O'Conor, a New York lawyer and reformer.

The Issues Two issues dominated the campaign. The first centered on the ongoing reconstruction of the southern states. The second was the call for reform and for the establishment of a sound civil service system that would hire government employees based on their merit, rather than their political support.

The Campaign The personalities of the candidates, more than the real issues, dominated the campaign. While Greeley was intelligent, he was also cranky, sloppy, and extravagant. He had a round face, big blue eyes, and a bald head, wore steel-rimmed glasses, and his appearance was ridiculed by the political cartoonists of the day. Most of the nation's newspapers criticized him. The *New York Times* noted that "If any one man could send a great nation to the dogs, that man is Greeley." Despite the corruption, most of the nation was prosperous. While Grant himself did not campaign, the Republican party "waved the bloody shirt."

The Democratic newspapers called Grant stupid, a drunk, a swindler, and a crook. He was

Henry Wilson (1812–1875) was born Jeremiah Jones Colbath, the son of a poor sawmill worker. At age ten, he was sent to a nearby farm, where he worked for more than ten years for no money, only room and board. In his free time, he educated himself by reading as many books as he could borrow. On his twenty-first birthday, Jeremiah was given his freedom and some livestock—six sheep and two oxen. He sold the animals for $85 and legally changed his name to Henry Wilson. He then walked for more than 100 miles to Natick, Massachusetts, where he apprenticed himself to a shoemaker. He quickly learned the trade and set up his own shop. By age 27, he owned a shoe factory that employed about 100 people. At the same time, he continued to educate himself. In 1840 he was elected to the Massachusetts legislature and in 1855 to the United States Senate, where he served until he became vice president in 1873. He strongly opposed slavery throughout his political career. Shortly after the 1872 election, Wilson suffered a stroke, but recovered shortly afterward. In 1875 he died from a second stroke.

attacked for the corruption in his administration and for allowing businesses and industries to grow richer, often by illegal means. Greeley hit the campaign trail in September 1872 and gave a series of speeches. He criticized the Republicans and called for reconciliation between the North and South. Some voters were impressed by Greeley's intelligence, but he often said things that turned veterans and African American voters against him.

The Election Grant won an overwhelming victory—286 **electoral votes** and 3,598,235 popular votes. Grant carried 31 of the 37 states.

Greeley won 2,834,761 popular votes and O'Conor 18,602. Greeley was completely crushed by his defeat. During the campaign, he had lost control of his newspaper, and his wife had died shortly before the election. Physically and mentally exhausted, Greeley died on November 29, 1872—before the electoral votes were counted.

Greeley's electors were confronted with a unique situation. They were pledged to vote for him, but could not vote for a dead man. Of Greeley's electors, 42 cast their vote for Thomas Hendricks of Indiana and 18 for Benjamin Gratz Brown, the Democratic vice-presidential candidate. Three cast votes for others and three did not vote. *See also* ELECTION OF 1868 (GRANT); ELECTION OF 1876 (HAYES).

In September 1872, less than two months before Grant's reelection, the New York *Sun* began to expose the Crédit Mobilier scandal. Beginning in the 1860s Congress gave vast amounts of money to several railroads, including the Union Pacific and the Central Pacific, to build a transcontinental railroad. The Union Pacific formed a construction company—the Crédit Mobilier of America—to build the railroad. The Union Pacific directors then became the directors of the construction firm. To swindle illegal profits, the Crédit Mobilier was paid as much as $50,000 per mile for construction, even though the actual cost was about $30,000. The directors and other stockholders shared the company's huge profits. To protect this scheme, shares were sold below their market value to members of Congress in return for legislative support. A congressional investigation showed that several members of Congress and Vice President Schuyler Colfax (1869–1873) had made huge sums of money through this scam.

Election of 1876

Rutherford B. Hayes ✪ Rutherford B. Hayes brought great experience to his election campaign. He won a tight victory in a heavily disputed election—one that almost led to a second civil war.

▲ Hayes was an honest and capable president.

The Candidates President Grant seriously considered running for a third term. But the corruption that plagued his administration caused him to lose some of his popularity, and many people—**Republicans** and **Democrats** alike—were opposed to anyone breaking the two-term tradition started by George Washington. After Grant decided to retire, several prominent Republicans wanted the nomination. Among them were James G. Blaine of Maine, Roscoe Conkling of New York, and Rutherford B. Hayes of Ohio. Blaine was the favorite at the Republican convention in Cincinnati, but the delegates **deadlocked** after the seventh **ballot**. Support quickly grew for Hayes and he won the nomination on the eighth ballot. For vice president, the Republicans selected William A. Wheeler, a congressman from New York.

When the Democrats met in St. Louis, two candidates struggled for the nomination. Samuel J. Tilden, the governor of New York, was well known for his honesty and reforms. Thomas A. Hendricks of Indiana was favored by the western states. Tilden proved more popular and was easily nominated for president on the first ballot. Hendricks received the number two spot on the **ticket**.

Two minor parties also ran candidates. The Independent National party nominated Peter Cooper for president and Samuel E. Cary for vice president. This party, nicknamed "green-

> • • • • • • • • • •
> **"Hurrah for Hayes and Honest Ways!"**
> —Campaign slogan praising Hayes's clean political record, 1876

backers," favored the printing of more paper money. The Prohibition Reform party wanted to ban the manufacturing and sales of alcohol. They chose Green Clay Smith for president and Gideon T. Stewart for vice president.

The Issues The main issue of the campaign was **reform**—changes and improvements in government. Both major parties favored it, especially a civil service system that would hire government employees based on merit, rather than on political support. The Democrats, attacking the corruption of the Grant administration, loudly called for reform. The Republicans, being careful not to criticize President Grant, were less outspoken. Other issues included a recent economic crisis, called the Panic of 1873, and the withdrawal of federal troops from the South.

The Campaign Because both major candidates favored reform and took similar stands on the other issues, supporters of both candidates resorted to **mudslinging** and personal attacks to try to win votes. Republican speakers and newspapers hit Tilden with a stream of false-hoods. They accused him of praising slavery, evading taxes, and making millions of dollars defending corrupt New York politicians. Tilden was called a liar, a thief, a drunk, and a swindler. Republicans also "waved the bloody shirt" and attacked the Democrats as having sided with the rebels during the Civil War.

The Democrats, too, flung lies. They claimed that Hayes stole the pay of dead soldiers during the Civil War, that he cheated Ohio out of great amounts of money as governor, and that he shot his mother in a fit of rage.

Both parties were well organized and spent vast sums on the campaign. Rallies included cannons, brass bands, fiery speeches, and plenty of food to sway voters. Yet both candidates stayed home, attending to their jobs as governors of their respective states. The election of 1876 was one of the closest and most hotly contested in the nation's history.

The Election After the voters cast their ballots on November 7, 1876, it looked as if Tilden had won. Many newspapers reported a Tilden victory, and Tilden himself was sure he had won. Hayes went to bed on the night of Election Day believing he had lost. It appeared that Tilden had won 184 **electoral votes**—1 short of the needed 185. Hayes had won 165 electoral votes. But the votes of Oregon, South Carolina, Louisiana, and Florida were in dispute. Tilden needed only 1 vote, but Hayes needed them all. Furthermore, Tilden won the popular vote—4,288,546 to Hayes's 4,034,311.

In the three former Confederate states, two sets of election returns were sent in—one favoring Hayes and one Tilden. In Oregon, one Republican elector was disqualified and both parties struggled for that one vote. Tensions flared as each side accused the other of trying to steal the election.

The Constitution offered little guidance. It simply states, "The President of the Senate

The Election of 1876

Party		Popular Vote	Electoral Vote
Hayes	Republican	4,036,311	165
Tilden	Democratic	4,288,546	184
Disputed			20
			369 Total

The disputed electoral votes of four states kept the outcome of the election of 1876 unclear until just before the inauguration.

shall, in the presence of the Senate and the House of Representatives, open all the certificates, and the votes shall be counted." So to resolve the crisis, Congress appointed a special fifteen-member electoral commission—five senators, five representatives, and five associate Supreme Court justices. The commission was to include seven Democrats, seven Republicans, and one independent. But five days before the commission was to meet, the independent, Associate Justice David Davis, resigned because he had been elected to the United States Senate from Illinois. Since all the remaining justices were Republicans, a Republican—Justice Joseph Bradley—replaced Davis and the commission's balance was tipped.

In February Congress met to start counting the electoral votes. The electoral commission reviewed each set of disputed returns and awarded them all to Hayes—the commission voting strictly along party lines. The final electoral vote was 185 for Hayes and 184 for Tilden.

Lucy Hayes (1831–1889), the daughter of a doctor, was the first First Lady to have a college degree. Her family had instilled in her a strong opposition to slavery. She met Rutherford B. Hayes in 1847 and married him in 1851. She took an active interest in her husband's military and political career and helped turn him against slavery. Lucy Hayes was very religious. After she became First Lady in 1877, she started daily morning worship in the White House. She also banned all alcoholic beverages from the White House, earning the nickname "Lemonade Lucy." Lucy began the tradition of the children's Easter Egg Roll on the White House lawn. After President Hayes's one term, the couple retired to Ohio in 1881. Lucy died there of a stroke in 1889.

Democrats were outraged and claimed fraud. In some states, Democrats began arming themselves. They shouted "Tilden or blood!" and "On to Washington!" Yet Tilden himself calmly accepted the commission's decision. His campaign manager said, " I prefer four years of Hayes's administration to four years of civil war."

While the electoral commission was still at work, a series of secret meetings between northern Republicans and southern Democrats took place. A compromise was reached. The Democrats would accept Hayes as president if he pledged to remove the remaining federal troops from the South, appoint a southerner to his cabinet, and support federal money for education and improvements in the South.

Soon after his inauguration on March 4, 1877, Hayes made good on his promises and Reconstruction came to an end. *See also* ELECTION OF 1868 (GRANT); ELECTION OF 1872 (GRANT); ELECTION OF 1880 (GARFIELD).

Election of 1880

James A. Garfield ✪ Garfield was a compromise candidate between two factions of the Republican party. He won the presidency in a very close election.

The Candidates President Hayes chose not to run for reelection in 1880. During his term, the **Republican party** split into two **factions**, or groups. The Stalwarts, led by Senator Roscoe Conkling of New York, favored the **spoils system** of patronage in which the winning party appointed political favorites to government jobs. The less radical Half-Breeds favored a civil service system in which people received government jobs based on their abilities. Maine senator James G. Blaine led the Half-Breeds. As the 1880 election approached, Conkling and the Stalwarts pushed to have former president Ulysses S. Grant nominated for a third term. The Half-Breeds, who recalled the corruption of the Grant administration, strongly opposed this idea.

At the Republican convention, the Stalwarts tried to force Grant's nomination. But the Half-Breeds countered with strong support for Blaine's candidacy. Secretary of the Treasury John Sherman also sought the nomination as a compromise candidate. Ohio Senator James A. Garfield, who supported the Half-Breeds, gave an impassioned speech to the convention calling for Sherman's nomination. He claimed Sherman was the only candidate who could unite the party. The delegates began voting and quickly became **deadlocked**—neither Grant, nor Blaine, nor Sherman had enough support to

> "My God, what is there in this place that a man should ever want to get into it?"
>
> —*James A. Garfield, shortly after taking office*

▲ Garfield served 199 days of his term as president.

win the nomination. During the early balloting, a few delegates had cast votes for Garfield. His support began to grow and finally, on the thirty-sixth **ballot**, Garfield won the nomination. To help unite the party, the convention nominated Chester A. Arthur of New York, a long-time political friend of Stalwart Roscoe Conkling, as vice president.

The Democrats, too, were divided, and several men wanted the nomination. Among them were Thomas F. Bayard of Delaware, Thomas A. Hendricks of Indiana, Henry B. Payne of Ohio, and General Winfield S. Hancock, a hero from the Battle of Gettysburg. On the second ballot, the delegates nominated Hancock, who had no government experience. For vice president, the Democrats chose millionaire banker William H. English of Indiana.

The Issues **Reform**, honest government, and the **tariff** were the issues of the day. The candidates shared similar views on most issues. The main difference was the tariff, or tax on imported goods. The Republicans favored a high tariff, but the Democrats called for a lower tariff to raise money for the government. Otherwise, the campaign centered on the private lives of the candidates.

The Campaign

Throughout the campaign, both parties boasted of the war heroism, honesty, and integrity of their candidates. The Republicans "waved the bloody shirt," but this had little effect. The Democrats reminded voters about the "fraud" from the ELECTION OF 1876, but this, too, did not stir voters.

The Democrats charged that Garfield had accepted $329 from Crédit Mobilier, a scandal-ridden company, during the Grant administration. Garfield pointed out this was a loan that had been paid back.

Because Hancock had no political background, the Republicans had little to criticize. One newspaper claimed that Hancock "does nothing but eat, drink, and enjoy himself." During the campaign, however, Hancock blundered when he told a newspaper reporter, "The tariff question is a local question." The Republican newspapers and cartoonists harassed Hancock and the Democrats because of this error.

Just weeks before the election a letter, supposedly signed by Garfield, that called for more Chinese immigrant workers to come to the United States surfaced in the news. Garfield and the Republicans claimed the letter was a forgery. But the Democrats kept printing copies of the letter, especially in California. At that time, most Californians strongly opposed

Chester A. Arthur (1830–1886) grew up in Vermont. As a lawyer, he often defended runaway slaves. Arthur became active in Republican politics around 1856. He then held several appointed posts in New York, including the powerful position of port collector of New York. He became vice president in 1880 without ever having won an elective office. Arthur assumed the presidency after President Garfield was assassinated in 1881. As president, Arthur signed the Pendleton Civil Service Reform Act in 1883. This law set up a commission to test and hire applicants for government jobs based on their qualifications, rather than their political connections. Arthur also worked to build the navy and reduce the national debt. After leaving office in 1885, Arthur returned to New York to practice law.

Chinese immigration. As a result of this fake letter, Garfield lost the votes of California—and almost the election.

The Election

When the votes were tallied, the popular vote was very close. Garfield had barely won a **plurality**, 4,446,158 popular votes (about 48.27 percent) to Hancock's 4,444,260 popular votes (48.25 percent). Of the **electoral vote**, Garfield won 214 to Hancock's 155. The divisions between North and South showed clearly. Garfield won every northern and western state except California, Nevada, and New Jersey. Hancock carried every former Confederate state.

Disaster struck on July 2, 1881, when Charles J. Guiteau shot Garfield as he waited to board a train in the Baltimore and Pacific Railroad station. After Guiteau fired, he shouted, "I am a Stalwart; now Arthur is president!" During the 1880 campaign, Guiteau had distributed Republican party materials and expected to receive a job as a diplomat. The repeated rejections from the White House had angered him, and he claimed to have received visions telling him to kill the president.

The president lingered with a bullet lodged near his spine, as doctors unsuccessfully tried to remove it. James Garfield died on September 19, 1881 and Chester A. Arthur became the twenty-first president. *See also* ELECTION OF 1872 (GRANT); ELECTION OF 1876 (HAYES); ELECTION OF 1884 (CLEVELAND).

Election **of 1884**

Grover Cleveland ✪ New York Governor Stephen
Grover Cleveland was the first Democrat to win the
presidency since 1856.

The Candidates **Republican incumbent**
Chester A. Arthur wanted to be nominated in
his own right for the presidency.
But James G. Blaine was the
favorite of the Republican party.
Although convention delegates at
first scattered their votes, Blaine
won the nomination on the fifth
ballot. For vice president, the
Republicans chose Senator John A.
Logan of Illinois, a former Civil
War general.

When the **Democrats** met in
Chicago, Grover Cleveland, the
reform governor of New York,
was the leading contender. He was nominated
on the second ballot. The Democrats' vice presidential choice was Thomas A. Hendricks of
Indiana. Hendricks had sought the presidency
several times before and was the vice-presidential candidate in the disputed election of 1876.

A group of reform-minded Republicans
called their own convention because they could
not support Blaine, who had a history of corruption. Rather than form a new party, they
decided to support Cleveland. The New York
Sun called them *mugwumps*, an Algonquin
Native American term meaning "great man."
The Mugwumps thought of themselves as
moral leaders who were more concerned with
helping the country than their political party.

The Issues As in 1880 there was little distinc-
tion between the candidates' views on the

▲ Cleveland is the only president to have served two nonconsecu-
tive terms.

- **"Ma! Ma!
Where's My
Pa?"**
  —*Republican criticism of
Democrat Grover Cleveland*

- **"Gone to the
White House.
Ha! Ha! Ha!"**
  —*Democratic response to the
Republicans*

major issues. The only real difference was that the Republicans
favored a higher **tariff** than did
the Democrats. As in the past two
elections, the campaign quickly
became a contest centered on the
moral integrity of the candidates.

The Campaign Democrats pointed
out Blaine's shady business deals,
some going back to before 1876.
Blaine had profited from using his
political influence to help the Little Rock and
Fort Smith Railroad. During the 1884 campaign, even more damaging stories leaked to
the media, including a note that closed with
"Burn this letter."

The Republicans in turn published a news
story that claimed that, while mayor of Buffalo,
Cleveland had fathered an illegitimate child.
When Cleveland's supporters asked what to
do, he told them, "Above all, tell the truth!"
Indeed, the story was true. His honesty helped
put the issue aside. Cleveland refused to campaign and instead stayed in the New York governor's office.

Blaine, on the other hand, campaigned
throughout the country and loved the people's
praise and applause. He attacked the Democrats
and the Mugwumps as "agents of foreign inter-
ests" who wanted to close mills and factories,

thus putting the average worker out of a job. The campaign looked close as election day drew near. But two events in New York City on October 29—three days before the election—probably cost Blaine the presidency. That morning a Presbyterian minister attacked the Democrats as the party of "Rum, Romanism, and Rebellion," meaning the party supported drinking alcoholic beverages, the Roman Catholic religion, and the South during the Civil War. Blaine did not dispute this claim. A reporter sent the news to Democratic headquarters. Cleveland's campaign managers printed thousands of flyers with the phrase and distributed them in Irish immigrant neighborhoods of New York City. The remark greatly offended the Irish, most of whom were Catholics. They came to view Blaine as anti-Catholic. As a result, these voters turned out in great numbers, casting their votes for Cleveland. The same evening Blaine and many of his wealthy supporters attended a fund-raising dinner in New York. The next morning, a political cartoon on the front page of the New York *World* read: "Blaine and the Money Kings." These events probably caused enough New York voters to switch their choice from Blaine to Cleveland, thus giving the Democrats a victory.

The Election When the votes were counted, Cleveland had won 48.5 percent of the popular votes and 219 **electoral votes**. Blaine earned 48.25 percent of the popular votes and 182 electoral votes. Blaine had lost New York by about 1,149 popular votes, and with it the election. *See also* ELECTION OF 1876 (HAYES); ELECTION OF 1880 (GARFIELD).

Frances Folsom Cleveland (1864–1947) was the daughter of a Buffalo, New York, attorney. One of the first people to see the infant Frances was Grover Cleveland, a close friend of her father. Grover Cleveland became her guardian after her father suddenly died in 1875. Shortly after Frances graduated from West College in Aurora, New York, Grover Cleveland proposed marriage. He had been a bachelor president for about two years, and was 49 years old. They married in the White House on June 2, 1886. At 21, Frances was the youngest First Lady. During her White House years, she was very popular with the people. She held public receptions on evenings or Saturdays so that working women could attend, which they did by the thousands. Her formal parties were also popular with Washington society. After the president's second term, the Clevelands retired to Princeton, New Jersey. Grover Cleveland died in 1908. A young widow, Frances later married a professor of archaeology from Princeton University. She was the first presidential widow to remarry. She died in 1947 and is buried next to President Cleveland in Princeton.

Election of 1888

Benjamin Harrison ✪ Benjamin Harrison ran his campaign from the front porch of his Indiana home. He won his home state by a slim majority of about 2,300 votes.

The Candidates Grover Cleveland, the **incumbent**, was the favorite for the **Democratic** nomination. He received his party's nod by **acclamation**. For vice president, the Democrats selected 75-year-old Allen G. Thurman, a former senator from Ohio.

As in 1884, James G. Blaine seemed to be the likely choice of the **Republicans**. Blaine suddenly withdrew from the contest, however, believing that an uncontested nomination would produce the best candidate to defeat President Cleveland. With Blaine officially out the race, several men sought the nomination. John Sherman of Ohio, Benjamin Harrison of Indiana, Russell Alger of Michigan, and William B. Allison of Iowa were among them. At first the delegates were divided and no one candidate seemed to be able to win the nomination. Some delegates wanted Blaine to reconsider, but he refused. But Blaine indicated he would support

- "Tippecanoe
- and Tariff,
- Too!"
- —*Republican campaign slogan referring to Benjamin Harrison's grandfather and the call for a high tariff, 1888*

▲ Benjamin Harrison was the grandson of the ninth president, William Henry Harrison (1841).

Harrison. Finally, on the eighth **ballot**, Harrison secured the nomination. The Republicans' vice presidential nominee was Levi P. Morton, a wealthy New York banker and former member of the House of Representatives.

The Issues The **tariff** was the main issue in the campaign. As in previous elections, the Republicans favored a higher tariff than did the Democrats.

The Campaign Neither candidate traveled or actively campaigned. Cleveland busied himself in the White House and would not allow his cabinet to campaign for him. Harrison received a steady flow of sup-

The 1888 Democratic candidates, Grover Cleveland and Allen G. Thurman, did not campaign.

Caroline Harrison (1832–1892) was born in Oxford, Ohio. She was well educated, artistic, and had musical talents as well. She met her future husband in 1848, and they married in 1853. When Caroline became First Lady in 1889, she hoped to rebuild the White House. She had three different plans drawn up, but Congress refused to approve them. She then began a remodeling plan that included repairing furniture, repainting, and adding bathrooms. Electricity was also installed in the White House during this time, although Caroline refused to touch the switches. Caroline's health grew worse during her time as First Lady. By 1892 she was very sick with tuberculosis, a deadly lung disease. Because Caroline was so ill, Benjamin Harrison refused to campaign during his reelection bid, as did his opponent, Grover Cleveland. Caroline died two weeks before the 1892 election, which her husband lost. She is buried in Indianapolis.

porters at his home in Indianapolis, where he gave carefully worded speeches. Blaine, still an important Republican leader, actively campaigned for Harrison and drew huge crowds wherever he went. Blaine pushed for the high tariff.

Compared to past campaigns, this one was quiet and free from most personal attacks. The Republicans did not raise the issue of Cleveland's illegitimate child but instead claimed that he beat his young wife. Mrs. Cleveland issued a statement that the charge was "a foolish campaign story."

The Election When the **electoral votes** were counted, Harrison had won a narrow victory in the **Electoral College** but had lost the popular vote. The Republican candidate earned 233 electoral votes to the Democrats' 168. But Cleveland had carried the popular vote—5,534,488 to Harrison's 5,443,892. *See also* ELECTION OF 1884 (CLEVELAND); ELECTION OF 1892 (CLEVELAND).

Election of 1892

The Candidates The **Republican** convention nominated **incumbent** Benjamin Harrison on the first **ballot**. For the second place on the **ticket**, the delegates passed over Vice President Levi Morton and chose Whitelaw Reid, the publisher of the New York *Tribune*.

▲ Grover Cleveland and his young wife, Frances, returned to the White House after four years.

When the **Democratic** convention met in Chicago, former president Grover Cleveland quickly became the favorite and was nominated on the first ballot. For vice president, the delegates chose former representative Adlai E. Stevenson of Illinois.

The Populist party, a new **third party**, nominated Civil War veterans James B. Weaver for president and James G. Field for vice president. This party called for several **reforms** and the return of government power to the "plain people."

The Issues As in recent campaigns, the Republicans favored a high **tariff** to protect the nation's industries. They also called for the unlimited coinage of silver, but only if other

> "Mr. Cleveland's triumph today has been largely due to the young voters. . ."
>
> —from the Nation, *a newspaper of the time*

industrial nations did so. The Democrats wanted a lower tariff, believing it should be used only to raise money for the government. They also opposed the unlimited coinage of silver. The Populists called for an income tax as well as public ownership of the railroads and the telegraph and telephone companies. They also called for an eight-hour workday and strongly supported coinage of silver to help farmers pay their debts.

The Campaign Neither Harrison nor Cleveland personally campaigned. Harrison stayed in the White House with Caroline, his very sick wife. She died two weeks before the election. Cleveland, partly out of respect for Harrison's personal situation, did not campaign. Both major candidates wrote letters of acceptance in which they

Election of 1892		
Candidate (Party)	Popular Vote	Electoral Vote
Grover Cleveland (Democrat)	5,551,883	277
Benjamin Harrison (Republican)	5,179,244	145
James B. Weaver (Populist)	1,024,280	22

⌢⌢⌢⌢⌢⌢⌢⌢⌢⌢⌢⌢⌢

ai E. Stevenson (1835–1914) was born to a slave-
ling family in Kentucky. When he was 16, the family
ed to Bloomington, Illinois, where Stevenson taught
ool and studied law. In 1858, he became a lawyer.
enson entered politics as a Democrat in 1864 and by 1874
elected to the United States House of Representatives. In
5 President Cleveland appointed Stevenson to be the first
stant postmaster. In this powerful position, he fired thou-
ls of postmasters who had been appointed by the previous
ublican administration, earning him the nickname "the
dsman." In 1892 the Democrats nominated Stevenson for
president. He and Cleveland easily defeated incumbent
jamin Harrison. Stevenson again was the choice for the
nd place on the Democratic ticket in 1900, running with
iam Jennings Bryan. The Democrats lost that year.
enson's grandson, Adlai E. Stevenson II, ran as the
ocratic presidential nominee in 1952 and 1956.

expressed their views, leaving the campaign trail to the vice-presidential candidates and other party leaders.

The Populist campaign took on
the fervor of a religious revival.
Populists, both women and men,
addressed huge rallies—often more
than 3,000 people. Two of the best-
known Populist speakers, Jerry
"Sockless" Simpson and Mary
"Yellin'" Lease, stirred the crowds into
a frenzy.

The Election On Election Day, Cleveland won with 277 **electoral votes** to
Harrison's 145 electoral votes. Populist
candidate Weaver won 22 electoral
votes, mostly from western farming
states. He was the first third-party
candidate to win any electoral votes
since the ELECTION OF 1860. *See also*
ELECTION OF 1884 (CLEVELAND);
ELECTION OF 1888 (HARRISON).

Election of 1896

William McKinley ✪ Republican William McKinley won the election of 1896, receiving more than 51 percent of the popular vote and 60 percent of the electoral vote.

The Candidates As the fall of 1896 approached, the **Republicans** were confident they would win the White House. Although several men wanted the nomination, William McKinley quickly became the favorite. McKinley had served in Congress and was the governor of Ohio when he was chosen. McKinley was a popular politician, but Mark Hanna, a rich Ohio business leader and Republican party leader, pushed his candidacy, exclaiming, "I love McKinley. He is the best man I ever knew." With Hanna's backing, McKinley won the nomination on the first **ballot**. For vice president, the Republicans chose Garret A. Hobart, a wealthy New Jersey business leader.

Several **Democrats** wanted the presidency. At first the leading candidate was Representative Richard Bland of Missouri. Other contenders included Robert E.

▲ McKinley conducted a "front porch" campaign from his home in Canton, Ohio.

> • "The Full
> • Dinner Pail"
> —Republican campaign
> slogan, 1896

"Free silver" refers to a late nineteenth-century movement that called for the federal government to mint an unlimited number of silver coins. Three key groups supported "free silver." The owners of silver mines wanted the government to buy their output. Farmers believed that having more silver coins in circulation would increase the price of their crops, while debtors thought that having additional silver coins would help them pay their debts more easily. The issue of "free silver" became a symbol of economic freedom for the average American. But the issue lost its luster after 1896, when good harvests and rising prices brought prosperity to farmers. New gold mines were discovered, and the world's supply of the precious metal doubled. Congress soon put the nation on the gold standard, enabling the Treasury Department to redeem all money in gold.

Pattison of Pennsylvania, Horace Boies of Iowa, and John R. McLean of Ohio. As the delegates started voting on their **platform**, William Jennings Bryan, a young former representative from Nebraska, called on the Democrats to help farmers and average workers by favoring the unlimited coinage of silver. He delivered a stirring speech, which closed with, "You shall not press down upon the brow of labor this crown of thorns, you shall not crucify mankind upon a cross of gold." Twenty thousand delegates jumped to their feet, shouting "Bryan! Bryan! Bryan!" At age 36, William Jennings Bryan became the Democrats' choice for the presidency, winning the nomination on the fifth ballot. For vice president, the delegates chose Arthur Sewall, a wealthy shipbuilder from Maine.

The Populists had gained popularity since the election of 1892. Their most important issue—the unlimited coinage of silver—was now part of the Democrats' platform. The Populists then nominated Bryan, the Democratic candidate, as their choice for president. For vice president, they nominated Thomas E. Watson, a well-known Populist.

The Issues The silver issue dominated the campaign. The Democrats and the Populists pushed to take the United States off the gold standard, claiming that unlimited coinage of silver would bring prosperity to workers throughout the country. The Republicans favored the gold standard and predicted that the unlimited coinage of silver would bring economic ruin to the nation.

The Campaign Bryan crossed the country in a highly spirited campaign—the most energetic up to that time. Sleeping only a few hours each night, he traveled about 18,000 miles in three months, addressing an estimated five million people. Bryan and other Democratic leaders called McKinley a "tool of the capitalists" who favored the wealthy over the average worker.

Ida McKinley (1847–1907) was the daughter of a wealthy Canton, Ohio, banker. After attending school, she worked in her father's bank because she wanted to, which was rare for a woman in the 1860s. While at the bank, she met William McKinley, whom she married in 1871. Tragedy struck the early years of their marriage. Ida's mother and the McKinleys' two young daughters died within two years. Ida never recovered from the shock; she became depressed and began having seizures. William McKinley was deeply devoted to his wife and tended to her every need. After his election, Ida was determined to be an active First Lady, despite her illness. The president changed the seating at formal dinners so that Ida could sit next to him. If she had a seizure, he would cover her face with his handkerchief until it had passed. After his assassination in 1901, she returned to Canton where she died in 1907.

Under the direction of his campaign manager Mark Hanna, McKinley stayed at his home in Canton, Ohio. From his front porch, he delivered well-rehearsed speeches to his supporters, who arrived in Canton almost daily. Republican party leaders spoke for McKinley across the nation. They also distributed millions of campaign flyers, many printed in foreign languages to attract the immigrant vote. The Republicans painted Bryan as a radical who would destroy the country. McKinley promised prosperity to the nation. Wealthy business owners gave millions of dollars to the Republican cause. As the election approached, some workers found slips of paper in their pay envelopes with the warning, "If Bryan is elected, do not come back to work. The plant will be closed."

The Election The well-organized and well-funded Republicans easily won the election. McKinley earned more than 7 million popular votes and 271 **electoral votes**. McKinley's support was mostly in the East and North. Bryan and the Democrats won about 6.5 million popular votes and 176 electoral votes, chiefly from the West and the South. *See also* ELECTION OF 1892 (CLEVELAND); ELECTION OF 1900 (MCKINLEY).

Election of 1900

William McKinley ✪ McKinley won an even bigger victory in the election of 1900 than he did in 1896, but only served about six months of his second term.

The Candidates The nation's prosperity and the American victory in the Spanish-American War (1898) assured President McKinley's popularity. The **Republican** convention renominated him on the first **ballot**. The delegates' attention focused on the vice-presidential nominee, as Vice President Hobart had died in 1899. After McKinley indicated he would accept whomever the delegates' selected, New York governor Theodore Roosevelt quickly became the favorite. Many delegates were impressed with Roosevelt's heroism in the Spanish-American War and with the **reforms** he was advocating in New York. But some political **bosses**, especially Thomas Platt of New York, supported Roosevelt's vice-presidential nomination because they wanted to get rid of the stubborn reform governor. Mark Hanna, McKinley's long-time friend and campaign manager, was horrified at Roosevelt's nomination. He shouted, "Don't any of you realize that there's only one

> • "Four More
> • Years of the
> • Full Dinner
> • Pail."
>
> —Republican campaign slogan, 1900

▲ McKinley became the third president to die at the hand of an assassin.

life between that madman and the presidency?"

As in 1896, the **Democrats** nominated William Jennings Bryan. For second place on the **ticket**, they chose Adlai E. Stevenson, vice president during Cleveland's second term.

The Issues The main issue of the campaign was imperialism. The United States annexed Hawaii in 1898 and, as a result of the Spanish-American War, the United States gained control of several Spanish colonies—Puerto Rico, Guam, and the Philippines. The Republicans favored keeping control of these lands until they could be "civilized." The Democrats favored granting independence to them as soon as possible.

The Campaign Following Mark Hanna's political advice, McKinley campaigned little. He stayed in the White House and

A 1900 campaign poster shows President McKinley measuring a growing Uncle Sam.

Tensions between the United States and Spain were mounting, when suddenly an American battleship, the *Maine*, blew up in Havana, Cuba's major harbor. Cuba was then a Spanish colony. The cause of the explosion was unknown, but many Americans and several newspapers blamed the Spanish. "Remember the *Maine*" became the nation's war cry. In April 1898, the United States declared war on Spain. By August, the war was over.

traveled occasionally to his home in Canton, Ohio. There he gave well-rehearsed speeches from his front porch, as he had done four years earlier. Hanna actively campaigned for the Republicans, crossing the nation and addressing crowds, even in areas where Bryan was popular. Theodore Roosevelt, too, hit the campaign trail, touring the country and giving several speeches a day. He delighted crowds with his outgoing personality and his brave reputation. Wherever he spoke, "Rough Riders"—fellow soldiers from the Spanish-American War—turned out to show their support.

As in 1896, Bryan traveled thousands of miles and spoke until he lost his voice. He criticized the Republican stand on imperialism and tried to again raise the issue of free silver—the unlimited minting of silver coins.

The Election On Election Day, McKinley and Roosevelt won almost 52 percent of the popular vote and 292 **electoral votes**. Bryan and Stevenson earned about 45 percent of the popular vote and 155 electoral votes.

On September 6, McKinley was

Mark Hanna (1837–1904), born Marcus Alonzo Hanna, was a prominent Cleveland industrialist who became a leader of the Ohio Republican party. His support helped McKinley gain the 1896 Republican presidential nomination. Hanna contributed about $100,000 of his own money to McKinley's campaign and raised an additional $3.5 million from other business leaders. In 1897, Hanna was appointed to the United States Senate. During the 1900 campaign, Hanna again raised millions of dollars for McKinley and the Republicans. Hanna remained in the Senate until his death in 1904. Some people thought Hanna would run for president before he died.

attending the Pan-American Exposition in Buffalo, New York. As he was shaking hands with well-wishers, Leon Czolgosz, an **anarchist**, approached the president with a bandage covering a revolver in his hand. As the president reached out to shake his other hand, Czolgosz fired two shots. Roosevelt, who had been on vacation, rushed to the president's bedside. After emergency surgery, McKinley seemed to improve greatly, and Roosevelt resumed his vacation. Less than a week later, on September 13, McKinley's condition worsened, and Roosevelt was summoned back to Buffalo. By the early morning of September 14, William McKinley was dead. Theodore Roosevelt, age 42, was now president. *See also* ELECTION OF 1896 (MCKINLEY); ELECTION OF 1904 (THEODORE ROOSEVELT).

Election of 1904

Theodore Roosevelt ✪ Theodore Roosevelt greatly wanted to be elected to the presidency. He won a landslide victory in the 1904 election.

The Candidates Theodore Roosevelt had become president in 1901, after William McKinley was assassinated. As the **incumbent**, he was popular throughout the country and had most of the **Republican party's** support. Nonetheless, Roosevelt wanted to win the presidency "in his own right." At the Republican convention in Chicago, he was nominated on the first **ballot**. For vice president, Roosevelt chose Charles W. Fairbanks, a senator from Indiana.

- "We Want
- Teddy for
- Four Years
- More"
- —Republican campaign
-   slogan, 1904

▲ At age 42, Roosevelt was the youngest man to assume the presidency.

"Teddy" Roosevelt was a national hero. In 1898, he had resigned his post as assistant secretary of the navy to fight in the Spanish-American War. He gained fame leading his troops, known as the "Rough Riders," up San Juan Hill in Cuba. Returning to the United States, Colonel Roosevelt again became involved in politics and was elected governor of New York in 1898. In 1900, he was the Republican convention's choice for vice president, and he assumed the presidency upon McKinley's death in 1901. Later, with the nation's entry into World War I (1914–1918), he offered to raise a force of volunteers, but President Wilson denied his request.

The **Democrats** did not have a candidate to match Roosevelt's fame. Former president Grover Cleveland and former candidate William Jennings Bryan refused to run. Instead, Cleveland endorsed Alton B. Parker, the chief justice of the New York Court of Appeals. Although Parker was unknown throughout the rest of the country, many other Democrats gave him

Born in 1858, Theodore Roosevelt was a sickly boy. His asthma made him cough so severely that he had to sleep sitting up. To build up his scrawny body, young Roosevelt began working out at a gym and then took boxing lessons. In his teens he led an active lifestyle.

Roosevelt studied at Harvard and then at Columbia Law School. A lawyer, he soon became involved in Republican politics and served in the New York State Assembly. After his first wife, Alice Hathaway Lee, died in 1884, Roosevelt quit politics and went west to the Dakota Badlands to become a rancher. In the "wild west," he continued his active lifestyle, regularly hunting, riding, fishing, and tending to chores. For a short time, he served as sheriff of Billings County in the Dakota Territory. After losing money on his ranch, Roosevelt moved back east. He then married his childhood sweetheart, Edith, and reentered politics.

Edith Roosevelt (1861–1948) grew up in the same neighborhood as her future husband, Theodore Roosevelt, and she was a close friend of his younger sister, Corrine. Edith did not attend college, but she was well read and intelligent. Roosevelt's first wife died in 1884 after a four-year marriage. Edith and Theodore married in 1886. They had five children. Edith was an active First Lady who often advised her husband. Concerned about her young family's privacy, Edith made sure the family's living quarters were separated from the offices when the White House was remodeled in 1902. To satisfy public curiosity, she provided the news media with photographs of her children. After leaving the White House with her husband in 1909, Edith retired to Oyster Bay, New York. She died in 1948 and is buried next to her husband.

their support, nominating him on the first ballot at the convention in St. Louis. Henry G. Davis, a former senator from West Virginia, was chosen for vice president. At 81, he was the oldest vice-presidential candidate ever nominated.

The Issues The hottest issues of recent elections had faded. Some Democrats who had supported Bryan in the past still favored "free silver." But Parker favored the gold standard. Similarly, most of the questions concerning imperialism had been settled—Cuba was granted independence and the other lands remained colonies. Both parties favored the rights of consumers and opposed **monopolies**—businesses without competition.

The Campaign With few contested issues at hand, the campaign was dull. Roosevelt and Parker agreed on most of the issues and neither candidate campaigned. Roosevelt stayed in the White House tending to the country's business. Parker ran a quiet front-porch campaign. As in the past, supporters and party loyalists spoke out for the candidates. Vice-presidential candidate Fairbanks campaigned in 33 states.

The Election On Election Day, Roosevelt won a huge victory—336 **electoral votes** to Parker's 140. The Republicans earned more than 2.5 million more popular votes than the Democrats. Roosevelt carried every northern and western state, while Parker won the South. *See also* ELECTION OF 1896 (MCKINLEY); ELECTION OF 1900 (MCKINLEY).

Election of 1908

The Candidates Soon after his election in 1904, Theodore Roosevelt declared that he would not run for reelection. To carry on his policies, he chose William Howard Taft, his friend and secretary of war. Convention delegates nominated Taft on the first **ballot**. For vice president, the **Republicans** selected Representative James S. Sherman of New York.

After their stunning defeat in 1904, the **Democrats** nominated William Jennings Bryan, their candidate in 1896 and 1900. For vice president, the Democrats nominated John W. Kern of Indiana, a friend of Bryan's who was unknown outside his home state.

> ● ● ● ● ● ●
> **"Shall the People Rule?"**
> —Democratic campaign slogan, 1908

The Issues Each party claimed that its candidate would better carry out Roosevelt's popular policies. Taft pledged to follow Roosevelt's plans. Bryan claimed that Roosevelt's policies were based on the Democrats' ideas and that he was the better candidate. The Democrats called for an eight-hour workday, a lower **tariff**, and the direct election of senators.

▲ Taft wanted to be chief justice of the United States more than he wanted to be president.

The Campaign At first, neither candidate actively campaigned. As the campaign heated up, however, both men traveled the country. Roosevelt advised Taft, "Hit them hard, old man. . . ." Taft attacked the Democrats' **platform** and predicted an economic crisis if Bryan were elected. During the campaign, Bryan declared that he favored public ownership of the railroads. As a result, he lost voter support.

The Election Taft easily won the election with 321 **electoral votes** to Bryan's 162. Taft earned about 7,670,000 popular votes to Bryan's 6,409,000. Bryan won the South and the western states of Nevada, Colorado, and Nebraska. Taft and the Republicans carried the rest of the country. *See also* ELECTION OF 1896 (MCKINLEY); ELECTION OF 1900 (MCKINLEY); ELECTION OF 1904 (THEODORE ROOSEVELT); ELECTION OF 1912 (WILSON).

Helen Taft (1861–1943) was born into a well-to-do family in Cincinnati, Ohio. Helen actively encouraged her husband to run for the presidency in 1908—without her push, he probably would not have done so. On Inauguration Day, she became the first First Lady to ride next to her husband. After four years in the White House, the Tafts retired to Connecticut. In 1921, they returned to Washington after William H. Taft was appointed chief justice. She remained in Washington after her husband's death in 1930. She died in 1943 and was buried next to her husband, becoming the first First Lady to be buried in Arlington National Cemetery.

Election of 1912

Woodrow Wilson ☸ Woodrow Wilson is the only president to earn a doctorate degree. Before entering politics, he had been a professor of political science and government at Princeton University.

The Candidates William H. Taft, the **incumbent**, sought the **Republican** nomination in 1912. He pointed to his successful record, claiming that he followed former President Theodore Roosevelt's policies as best as he could. He had the support of most of the Republican party, but he was not nearly as popular as Roosevelt had been. The former president and his **progressive** followers felt let down by Taft. They believed that Taft—despite his claims—did not hold strongly to Roosevelt's views. The party became divided between followers of Taft and supporters of Roosevelt. Even before the Republican convention met, Roosevelt declared, "My hat is in the ring." He ran in several **primary elections** and challenged Taft to do so. When reminded of his 1905 statement that he would not seek a third term, he explained that he meant he would not seek three terms in a row.

Taft and his supporters controlled the Republican party. When the convention met in Chicago, Taft's was the only name put forward. He easily won the nomination on the first **ballot**. James S. Sherman was again chosen for the vice presidency.

Furious, Roosevelt and his followers bolted the convention. They formed their own party, called the **Progressive party**. They met in August and nominated Roosevelt for president and Hiram Johnson, the governor of California, for vice president. The Progressive party became known as the Bull Moose party because

> - **"I'm feeling as fit as a bull moose!"**
> - —*Progressive candidate Theodore Roosevelt, 1912*

▲ Wilson became the first Democratic president since Grover Cleveland in 1892.

Roosevelt told reporters that he was feeling "fit as a bull moose."

Several **Democrats** were contenders for the presidential nomination. Among them were Speaker of the House Champ Clark of Missouri, Representative Oscar Underwood of Alabama, and Governor Judson Harmon of Ohio. But the strongest candidate was Woodrow Wilson, the **reform** governor of New Jersey. For days, no candidate could secure the nomination. Finally, on the forty-sixth ballot, Wilson was chosen. For vice president, the Democrats selected Thomas R. Marshall of Indiana.

The Issues Wilson and the Democrats promised the voters a program known as the New Freedom. They pledged to end monopolies, restore competition in the market, and establish the right of workers to **collective bargaining**. Roosevelt, in turn, offered a plan called the New Nationalism, which promised the federal regulation of business and a social welfare program. Taft and the other Republicans kept to the party **platform** and pointed to the successes of the administration.

The Campaign Because the Republicans were badly divided, Wilson was almost assured victory. Nonetheless, Wilson and Roosevelt energetically traveled across the country making speeches and seeking votes. Taft gave a few

Ellen Wilson (1860–1914) was born in Savannah, Georgia. Her father, a Presbyterian minister, saw to it that she had a good education. She studied art at Rome Female College in Georgia and painted throughout her life. Her work was displayed at a one-woman show in 1913. She met Woodrow Wilson in 1883 while still living at home, and he proposed within five months. After they married in 1885, they moved to several different colleges because of Woodrow's career as a professor. Ellen became one of his most trusted advisors after he entered politics. As First Lady, she kept a busy social schedule and was active in charity work. Sadly, she became terminally ill with a kidney ailment known as Bright's disease. Her health grew worse during 1913, and she died on August 6, 1914.

campaign speeches, but spent most of his time in the White House.

Wilson and Roosevelt quickly became the two major contenders. Wilson called for free competition in business and more free enterprise. Roosevelt called for government regulation of big business and fair wages for workers, including women. Wilson and Roosevelt competed over who was the most reform-minded candidate.

The Election With Republican votes divided, Wilson won the election. Wilson won 435 electoral votes to Roosevelt's 88 and Taft's 8. Wilson won a **plurality** of the popular vote—about 6,283,000 to Roosevelt's 4,119,000 and Taft's 3,486,000. When some of Wilson's students from Princeton came over to congratulate him, he told them, "I myself have no feeling of triumph tonight. I have a feeling of solemn responsibility." *See also* ELECTION OF 1904 (THEODORE ROOSEVELT); ELECTION OF 1908 (TAFT); ELECTION OF 1916 (WILSON).

The Election of 1912

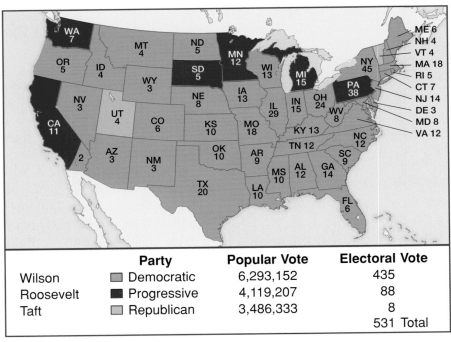

	Party	Popular Vote	Electoral Vote
Wilson	▨ Democratic	6,293,152	435
Roosevelt	■ Progressive	4,119,207	88
Taft	▫ Republican	3,486,333	8
			531 Total

The sharp divisions in the Republican party helped assure Democrat Woodrow Wilson's victory in the election of 1912.

Election of 1916

Woodrow Wilson ✪ Wilson's campaign pledged to keep the United States out of World War I, which was then raging in Europe. But in April 1917, Wilson asked Congress to declare war.

The Candidates As the election approached, it was clear that the **Democrats** would nominate President Woodrow Wilson for a second term. He fulfilled his campaign promises and kept the United States out of World War I (1914–1918), which was devastating Europe. Up to that time, the United States had an **isolationist**

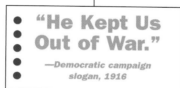

▶ "He Kept Us Out of War."
—Democratic campaign slogan, 1916

▲ Wilson's second-term victory was one of the closest elections in history.

foreign policy, meaning that it tried to keep out of other nations' wars. At the Democratic convention, Wilson was chosen on the first **ballot**. For vice president, the Democrats renominated Thomas R. Marshall of Indiana.

The favorite **Republican** candidate was New Yorker Charles Evans Hughes, who had been appointed to the United States Supreme Court by President William Howard Taft. Hughes won the nomination on the third ballot. He then resigned from the Court. For second place on the **ticket**, the Republicans nominated Theodore Roosevelt's vice president, Charles W. Fairbanks.

The Issues The war in Europe dominated the campaign. Both parties promised peace and pledged to build up the military in case of war.

The Campaign Wilson himself refused to campaign. Instead, he noted, "This is exactly what the people want. They want the President at a time like this to stay on his job." Loyal Democrats across the country campaigned on Wilson's behalf, noting that he had kept his campaign promises, and that the nation was prosperous and at peace.

Hughes campaigned vigorously, criticizing Wilson on war preparedness and relations with

When World War I broke out in Europe in August 1914, President Wilson declared America **neutral**. In other words, the United States would not take sides in the conflict. However, most Americans seemed to favor the British, partly because of a shared heritage, language, and culture. In addition, part of the German war strategy was to prevent ships carrying supplies from reaching Britain. Often German submarines, known as U-boats, sank ships in British waters without warning. Wilson warned the Germans that this practice might lead to war with the United States. Then on March 18, 1917, Germany sank three American ships, and Wilson asked Congress for a declaration of war. According to Wilson, the United States entered the war "to make the world safe for democracy." The war ended on November 11, 1918.

Mexico. Hughes called for a stronger national defense, a higher **tariff**, and a ban on child labor. Former President Roosevelt, too, attacked Wilson for not protecting American workers.

In the last days of the campaign, the Democrats blanketed the country with posters and slogans. "You are working—not fighting!" read one. "Wilson and peace with honor." read another. And one poster noted, "Alive and happy—not cannon fodder!"

The Election The election of 1916 is one of the closest in history. Hughes appeared to be the favorite, and early election returns from the East seemed to confirm his victory. By election night, Hughes had 254 **electoral votes** of the 266 needed to win. But the votes of California were being counted slowly. Because a Democrat had not won

---

Edith Wilson (1872–1961) had little formal schooling, receiving most of her education at home. She married Norman Galt, a jeweler. He died suddenly in 1908 and left Edith the business, which she continued to run successfully. In March 1915, Edith was introduced to Woodrow Wilson by his cousin, Helen Bones. They immediately fell for each other and married in December 1915. The new Mrs. Wilson brought life and cheer to the White House, and she became a trusted assistant to the president. After Woodrow was paralyzed by a stroke in October 1919, she completely protected him. While he recovered, she screened all official papers and business and selected the few visitors who could see the president. For a time, no one saw the president except Edith. Some critics claim she was really "acting president" during this time. To this day, no one knows for sure how much power Edith held, although she claimed that the president always made the important decisions. After Woodrow's death in 1924, she lived in Washington, traveled, wrote her memoirs, and directed the Woodrow Wilson Foundation. She died in 1961 and is buried next to her husband in Washington's National Cathedral.

California in 24 years, many experts believed that Hughes would carry California and thus win the presidency. Two days after the election, Hughes went to take a nap, telling his staff that he was not to be disturbed. But a reporter called and asked to speak to Hughes. His secretary replied that, "The president-elect is sleeping and cannot be disturbed." The reporter protested, "All right, but when Hughes wakes up tell him that he isn't the president-elect. The final returns from California just came in, and Wilson carried the state by about 3,400 votes."

Thus, Wilson won reelection with an electoral vote of 277 to Hughes's 254. Wilson won the popular vote by about a little more than 579,000 votes. *See also* ELECTION OF 1912 (WILSON).

Election of 1920

Warren G. Harding
⊙ Harding did not seek the presidency and did not expect to win the Republican nomination in 1920.

▲ Harding died of a stroke in August 1923.

The Candidates The **Republicans** were confident of victory in the 1920 election, and several candidates were considered. Among them were Theodore Roosevelt's friend General Leonard Wood, Governor Frank Lowden of Illinois, and Governor Hiram Johnson of California. Long-shot candidates included Governor Calvin Coolidge of Massachusetts, wartime food administrator Herbert Hoover, and Senator Warren G. Harding of Ohio. No candidate won enough delegates in the **primary elections** to secure the nomination. The convention became **deadlocked**. Party **bosses** met during the night and decided on Harding. The next morning, on the tenth **ballot**, Harding won the nomination. For vice president, the Republicans chose Calvin Coolidge.

Three candidates wanted the **Democratic** nomination. They were William Gibbs McAdoo, Woodrow Wilson's son-in-law and former secretary of the treasury, Attorney General A. Palmer Mitchell, and Governor James M. Cox of Ohio.

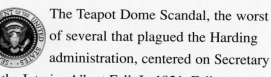

"**Return to Normalcy.**"
—Republican campaign slogan, 1920

Finally, after 44 ballots, the Democrats chose Cox. For the second place on the **ticket**, they selected Franklin D. Roosevelt, the assistant secretary of the navy.

The Issues The main issue was membership in the **League of Nations**. The League was President Wilson's dream—an international organization where countries could peacefully work out their differences. He insisted it become part of the Treaty of Versailles, which ended World War I. The Democrats favored membership in the League. On the other hand, the Republicans were generally opposed to the League, claiming that membership would hinder the nation's independence.

The Campaign Harding believed that life in America should return to the way it was before World War I (1914–1918). A few weeks before his nomination, he stated his

The Teapot Dome Scandal, the worst of several that plagued the Harding administration, centered on Secretary of the Interior Albert Fall. In 1921, Fall convinced Harding to transfer the control of naval oil reserves from the navy to the Department of the Interior. Fall then leased the reserves in Teapot Dome, Wyoming, to two oil executives for private use. In return, Fall received a $100,000 loan, $233,000 in government bonds, and $85,000 cash. Later, after the news of the scandal leaked, Fall was convicted of bribery, fined $100,000, and was jailed for one year, making him the first Cabinet officer to go to prison.

Florence Harding (1860–1924) was born into a wealthy family in Marion, Ohio. She attended local schools and then went to the Cincinnati Conservatory of Music. In 1880, she eloped with Henry De Wolf, with whom she had a child. De Wolf abandoned his young family, and in 1886 Florence divorced him. She met Warren G. Harding in 1890 and married him one year later. Florence took charge of the Harding household and turned Warren's newspaper into a profitable business. She pushed his political career, helping him win a United States Senate seat in 1914 and the presidency in 1920. As First Lady, Florence entertained lavishly. She opened the White House to the public and often visited wounded war veterans. After her husband's sudden death in 1923, she returned to Marion. She died there 15 months later and is buried in Marion next to her husband.

position: "America's present need is not heroics, but healing; not nostrums (medicines), but normalcy; not revolution, but restoration." The word *normalcy*, coined by Harding, was not proper English. Like several traditional Republican candidates before him, Harding ran a front-porch campaign in his hometown of Marion, Ohio, giving speeches to loyal Republicans. In contrast, Cox traveled about 22,000 miles, giving nearly 400 speeches. He supported the League of Nations and called on Americans to stay active in world affairs. He also wanted the nation to tackle its domestic problems, including illiteracy and poverty.

The Election Harding won by a landslide—404 **electoral votes** to Cox's 127. In the popular vote, the Republicans scored about 16,152,000 votes to the Democrats' 9,147,000. The election of 1920 was the first presidential election in which women could vote, as the Nineteenth Amendment had been **ratified** earlier in 1920. Sadly, Warren G. Harding died of a stroke after serving only two years and 151 days of his term. *See also* ELECTION OF 1916 (WILSON); ELECTION OF 1924 (COOLIDGE).

Election of 1924

Calvin Coolidge ✪ Calvin Coolidge became president after Warren G. Harding died in 1923. Coolidge was then elected in his own right in 1924.

The Candidates President Calvin Coolidge was nominated on the first **ballot**. For vice president, the **Republicans** chose Charles G. Dawes of Illinois, who had been the first budget director under Harding.

The **Democrats** were deeply divided by one major issue—the Ku Klux Klan, an organization promoting racial and religious hatred. In the early 1920s, the Klan had been gaining power in the South and the West, the strongholds of the Democratic party. Eastern Democrats wanted the party to completely reject the Klan. But many southern and western Democrats either supported the Klan or preferred to ignore it.

The convention delegates were almost evenly divided between two candidates. The East favored Alfred Smith, the liberal Catholic governor of New York. The West and the South supported William Gibbs McAdoo,

▲ Conservative and quiet, Coolidge was known as "Silent Cal."

> "Keep Cool with Coolidge."
>
> —Republican campaign slogan, 1924

Grace Coolidge (1879–1957), an only child, was born to a well-established New England family. She attended public schools and graduated from the University of Vermont in 1902. She then taught at the Clarke Institute for the Deaf in Northampton, Vermont. She met Calvin Coolidge in 1903, and they married two years later. The Coolidges had two sons, one of whom died at age 16 at the White House in 1924. Grace Coolidge was a very popular First Lady; she loved baseball, music, and theater. Grace lived 24 years longer than her husband. During those years, she raised millions of dollars for the Clarke Institute and worked to improve the lot of the hearing-impaired. During World War II, she worked with the Red Cross. She died in 1957 and was buried next to her husband and her son in Plymouth Notch, Vermont.

even though he publicly rejected the Klan. Ballot after ballot was taken, but neither man could reach the two-thirds **majority** needed for the nomination. Finally on the 103rd ballot, the delegates nominated **dark horse** John W. Davis, a law professor, West Virginia politician, and former minister to Great Britain. For vice president the Democrats chose Nebraska governor Charles W. Bryan, the brother of three-time presidential candidate William Jennings Bryan.

The **Progressive party** nominated Senator Robert M. La Follette of Wisconsin. Burton K. Wheeler, a Montana senator, was selected as the vice-presidential candidate.

The Issues The Republicans pointed to the strong economy and the prosperity of the nation. The Democrats reminded voters about Teapot Dome and other scandals of the Harding administration and criticized Coolidge. La Follette and the Progressives called for government ownership of all transportation, the election of federal judges, low **tariffs**, and environmental conservation.

The Campaign Coolidge spent most of the time in Washington, D.C. As he explained, "I don't recall any candidate for president that ever injured himself very much by not talking." As in the past, Republican loyalists traveled across the country, praising Coolidge and the prosperity of the nation. In contrast, Democrat Davis campaigned vigorously. He supported the Democratic platform and denounced the Klan. He tried to blame the scandals of the Harding administration on Coolidge, but he stirred little interest. La Follette, too, traveled the nation, giving 20 speeches in 13 states. The nation was not in the mood for **reform**, or change.

The Election The election was a Republican landslide, with Coolidge winning 382 **electoral votes** to Davis's 136 and La Follette's 13. Coolidge won 54 percent of the popular vote, compared with 29 percent for Davis and 17 percent for La Follette. Coolidge carried every northern and western state, except La Follette's home state of Wisconsin. Davis won every southern state. *See also* ELECTION OF 1920 (HARDING); ELECTION OF 1928 (HOOVER).

Election of 1924		
Candidate (Party)	*Popular Vote*	*Electoral Vote*
Calvin Coolidge (Republican)	15,719,921	382
John W. Davis (Democrat)	8,386,704	136
Robert M. La Follette (Progressive)	4,832,532	13

Election of 1928

Herbert C. Hoover ✪ Republican Herbert C. Hoover promised continued prosperity. Within his first nine months in office, however, the worst economic crisis in the nation's history—the Great Depression—brought poverty and unemployment.

The Candidates President Coolidge was very popular and could have easily won the **Republican** nomination and the presidency in 1928. In late 1927, however, he handed reporters a slip of paper that read: "I do not choose to run for president in nineteen twenty-eight." With Coolidge out of the running, Herbert C. Hoover quickly became the Republican favorite. Hoover had headed the American Relief Committee in Europe during World War I and was secretary of commerce in the Harding and Coolidge administrations. When the convention met in Kansas City, Hoover won the nomination on the first **ballot**. For vice president, the Republicans selected Senator Charles Curtis of Kansas, the first candidate who was part Native American.

The **Democratic** Convention, which met in Houston, quickly rallied around a popular candidate—New York governor Alfred Smith, nicknamed "the happy warrior." As their vice-presidential nominee, the Democrats chose Arkansas Senator Joseph E. Robinson.

▲ Herbert C. Hoover was the first president born west of the Mississippi River.

> ● "A Chicken
> ● in Every
> ● Pot and a
> ● Car in Every
> ● Garage."
> *—Republican campaign slogan, 1928*

The Issues Two issues dominated the campaign—religion and **Prohibition**. Al Smith was Roman Catholic. At the time, many Americans were prejudiced against Catholics. They feared that the pope in Rome would control a Catholic president and that Catholicism might become the national religion. Prohibition, the practice of forbidding the production, transportation, or sale of alcoholic beverages, had become the law of the land in 1920. This issue greatly divided the country. Many northern and eastern Democrats and city dwellers were against prohibition. On the other hand, most Republicans and many southern Protestant Democrats favored it.

The Campaign Hoover actively campaigned on the Republicans' record of economic prosperity. He also stated that prohibition, "a great social and economic experiment," must be strictly enforced. The Republicans

Election of 1928		
Candidate (Party)	*Popular Vote*	*Electoral Vote*
Herbert C. Hoover (Republican)	21,437,277	444
Alfred E. Smith (Democrat)	15,007,698	87

Lou Hoover (1874–1944) was born in Iowa and attended public schools there until 1884, when she and her family moved to California. She later enrolled at Stanford University and majored in geology, the first woman to do so. An intelligent woman, Lou spoke five languages fluently. At Stanford, she met Herbert Hoover, also a geology student. They married in 1899 and moved to China, where Herbert had a job with a mining firm. They next moved to Great Britain. During World War I, she helped Herbert, then in charge of the Wartime Food Administration, to feed the people of war-torn Europe. When she moved to the White House in 1929, Lou was more politically active than recent First Ladies. She gave radio addresses from the White House, supported social causes and women's rights, and served as president of the Girl Scouts of America. When the Great Depression began, she put the White House on a tight budget. She donated very liberally to charities, yet kept her generosity from the public. Not even her husband knew how many people she had helped until after her death in 1944, when he went through her papers.

criticized Smith for his lack of foreign-policy experience.

Smith and the Democrats raised Teapot Dome and other scandals from the Harding administration. They claimed that the Republican prosperity was bought at the expense of the average worker. On the prohibition issue, Smith favored modifying the laws to let the states decide whether to allow light beer and wine.

For the first time, both candidates traveled extensively by car throughout the country. As city motorcades drove through busy main streets, the candidates were able to reach more voters than ever before. Smith, clever and quick-witted, came across to voters as pleasant and easy going. The academic Hoover, in contrast, was seen as dull and lackluster. Yet Smith's good nature could not convince the voters to elect him.

The Election On Election Day, Hoover scored a landslide—444 **electoral votes** to Smith's 87. Hoover won 40 of the 48 states, including Smith's home state of New York. Smith carried two New England states—Massachusetts and Rhode Island—and six states in the Deep South—Arkansas, Louisiana, Mississippi, Alabama, Georgia, and South Carolina. *See also* ELECTION OF 1924 (COOLIDGE); ELECTION OF 1932 (FRANKLIN D. ROOSEVELT).

Election of 1932

Franklin D. Roosevelt ✪ Franklin D. Roosevelt won a landslide victory, carrying all but six states and defeating Herbert Hoover by more than seven million votes. By 1932, the country was looking for new leadership to help end the severe economic problems of the Great Depression.

▲ Franklin D. Roosevelt was the only president to serve more than two terms (1933–1945).

The Candidates **Republican** Herbert Hoover, the **incumbent**, chose to run for reelection in 1932. Having won an outstanding victory in the election of 1928, he promised that the good times of the 1920s would continue. Within months of taking office, however, economic disaster struck. In October 1929, the stock market crashed and thousands of people lost their life savings. Soon businesses were closing, and many of the nation's workers lost their jobs. The unemployment rate reached 25 percent. Without money, people could not pay their mortgages or other bills, and many families became homeless.

President Hoover tried to end what became known as the Great Depression by asking businesses not to lay off workers. He also asked private charities to help the homeless and unemployed. These efforts did not work. As the Depression grew worse, people called for help from the federal government. Hoover, however, believed that the government should not interfere in the economy. In spite of these problems, the

> ● **"The only thing we have to fear is fear itself."**
> ●
> —*Franklin D. Roosevelt,*
> *First Inaugural Address,*
> *March 4, 1933*

Republicans renominated Hoover on the first **ballot** and Vice President Charles Curtis was again chosen for second place on the **ticket**.

The **Democrats** realized that new leadership was needed to help the country. Several men wanted the presidential nomination, believing they could help improve the nation's economy. Franklin Delano Roosevelt, the governor of New York, quickly became the **front-runner**. Roosevelt was a progressive leader whose economic recovery plans were beginning to help his home state. The Democratic Convention, held in Chicago, nominated Roosevelt on the fourth ballot. For vice president, the Democrats selected Texan John Nance Garner, the Speaker of the United States House of Representatives.

Roosevelt flew to Chicago to accept the nomination—the first candidate to do so. He wanted to show that his physical disability would not interfere

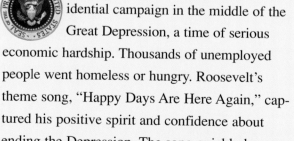

Franklin D. Roosevelt started his presidential campaign in the middle of the Great Depression, a time of serious economic hardship. Thousands of unemployed people went homeless or hungry. Roosevelt's theme song, "Happy Days Are Here Again," captured his positive spirit and confidence about ending the Depression. The song quickly became a favorite of the Democratic party, and it is still played at every Democratic convention.

with his duties as president. In 1921, Roosevelt had contracted infantile paralysis, or polio. The disease left him paralyzed from the waist down; he could walk only with the help of an aide and heavy leg braces. In private, he used a wheelchair to get around.

The Issues With so many people unemployed, hungry, or homeless, the nation's economy was the major issue of the campaign. The voters wanted the Great Depression to end quickly so they could get back to work. In addition, many voters wanted to end **Prohibition**, the practice of forbidding the production, transportation, or sale of alcoholic beverages. Prohibition, which had begun in 1920, had led to a sharp rise in organized crime, as bootleggers and gangsters illegally made and sold liquor.

The Campaign With President Hoover and the Republicans unpopular, the Democrats were sure of victory. Roosevelt called for a "new deal for the American people." He promised unemployment relief, support for farmers, old-age insurance, a **balanced federal budget**, and an end to Prohibition. Roosevelt campaigned across the country, reaching out to everyday men and women. He was warmly received.

Eleanor Roosevelt (1884–1962) was born into a distinguished New York family, but her mother died when she was young. A shy girl, Eleanor was raised by a strict great aunt and taught by tutors. She married her distant cousin Franklin Roosevelt in 1905. Eleanor's uncle, President Theodore Roosevelt, gave her away at the wedding. After Franklin contracted polio in 1921, Eleanor began to travel and make public appearances on his behalf. When she became First Lady in 1933, she became Franklin's "eyes and ears." She went to coal mines, factories, and farms. She brought information back to the president and worked for programs that helped the poor and unemployed. One of the most active First Ladies, she also helped expand employment opportunities for women and African Americans. After President Roosevelt died in 1945, she continued to work for human rights.

Hoover stood by his record and gave only ten speeches. He tried to blame the nation's economic problems on foreign causes and offered no concrete plans to halt the Depression. He also said that Prohibition should be left up to the states. Unpopular, Hoover often faced hostile audiences and was sometimes booed by the crowds.

Both parties also used **smear tactics** in the campaign. The Democrats tried to tarnish Hoover's reputation, saying he was a German sympathizer during World War I and that he made millions of dollars in crooked financial schemes. The Republicans attacked Roosevelt's health. They also said that if the Democrats won the election, those who still had jobs would lose them.

The Election On Election Day, Roosevelt won 42 states with 472 **electoral votes**. Hoover carried only 6 states with 59 votes. Roosevelt beat Hoover by more than 7 million popular votes—one of the largest wins up to that time. *See also* ELECTION OF 1920 (HARDING); ELECTION OF 1928 (HOOVER); ELECTION OF 1936 (FRANKLIN D. ROOSEVELT); ELECTION OF 1940 (FRANKLIN D. ROOSEVELT); ELECTION OF 1944 (FRANKLIN D. ROOSEVELT).

Election of 1936

Franklin D. Roosevelt ✪ Roosevelt won reelection in one of the most one-sided elections in history. The Democratic ticket won more than 60 percent of the popular vote and 98 percent of the electoral vote.

The Candidates As president, Franklin D. Roosevelt worked to bring economic recovery to the country, still struggling from the hardships of the Great Depression. His economic and social program, known as the New Deal, reached every part of society—the unemployed, the elderly, businesses, and farmers. He worked closely with Congress to pass laws that created new federal agencies. Among these were the Works Progress Administration (WPA), which stimulated businesses; the National Recovery Act (NRA), which increased industrial production; and the Agricultural Adjustment Act (AAA), which helped farmers. In 1935, Congress passed the Social Security Act, one of the most important laws in the country's history. This law provided unemployment insurance, some welfare assistance, and a monthly retirement benefit to people who stopped working at age 65. The lives of people

▲ Roosevelt did not let his disability keep him from being a great leader.

> "This generation of Americans has a rendezvous with destiny."
>
> —Franklin D. Roosevelt, nomination acceptance speech, 1936

John Nance Garner (1868–1967) was born in rural Texas. He won a seat in the United States House of Representatives in 1902. He served in the House until 1933, becoming Speaker in 1931. Garner wanted the Democratic presidential nomination in 1932. At the convention, however, after the third **deadlocked** ballot, Garner threw his support to Roosevelt. Roosevelt then supported Garner for vice president. The same ticket was reelected in a 1936 landslide. Garner opposed Roosevelt's running for a third term in 1940. Garner retired from politics in 1940 and returned to Texas where he died in 1967, two weeks before his ninety-ninth birthday. He lived longer than any other president or vice president.

throughout the nation were improved because of the New Deal. Thus, as the election of 1936 approached, Roosevelt was enormously popular and assured of the nomination. He was chosen by **acclamation**, and Vice President John Nance Garner was again selected for second place on the **ticket**.

Among the **Republicans**, several men wanted the nomination, but Governor Alfred M. Landon of Kansas quickly emerged as the leading contender. Former president Herbert Hoover had hoped for the nomination but gained little support from party leaders. At the Republican convention, Landon won the nomination on the first **ballot**. For vice president, the Republicans chose Frank Knox, a newspaper publisher.

President Franklin D. Roosevelt helped calm the nation's fears with weekly radio addresses.

The Issues The main issue of the campaign was economic recovery. The **Democrats** pointed to the success of the New Deal and the economic improvements of the past four years. Landon, at least at first, approved of the goals of the New Deal, but opposed the president's means. The **Prohibition** issue, which had so divided the country in the ELECTION OF 1932, was resolved by the passage of the Twenty-first Amendment to the Constitution. This amendment repealed the Eighteenth Amendment, leaving the decision about the manufacture and sale of alcohol to the states.

The Campaign Landon traveled on four national campaign tours. In the beginning, he attacked President Roosevelt's methods concerning economic recovery. He claimed that New Deal programs wasted money, were poorly run, and that they were against businesses. On the fourth tour, he charged that Roosevelt and the New Deal were "strangling free enterprise" and that the election was a battle to save the American system of government. The Republicans also attacked Social Security, which was to go into

effect on January 1, 1937. They charged that it was a "gigantic swindle" and a "pay reduction" for American workers.

At the start of the campaign, Roosevelt stayed in the White House and then took a sailing vacation. In October, however, Roosevelt struck out with both personal appearances and radio addresses. He defended the New Deal and pointed out that Americans—farmers, workers, and business leaders—were all better off in 1936 than they had been in 1932. Roosevelt attracted huge crowds wherever he went. In Chicago, admirers lined five miles of streets and 100,000 people filled the Chicago Stadium to hear him speak.

Interestingly, the *Literary Digest*, a popular magazine of the time, predicted a big Landon win. The magazine boasted it was going to "settle November's election in October." The *Digest* had correctly forecasted the winners of the 1920, 1924, 1928, and 1932 elections. But this time, the *Digest* had sent its postcards—used to conduct the **poll**—to automobile owners and people listed in the telephone books. Voters who were hardest hit by the Great Depression—and unlikely to have a phone or own a car—were not included in the poll. Because the *Digest* did not accurately sample eligible voters, they concluded that Landon would win 370 **electoral votes** to Roosevelt's 161. They could not have been more wrong. The *Digest* went out of business.

The Election On Election Day, Roosevelt won a stunning reelection victory. The Democrats won 523 **electoral votes** and more than 27,757,000 popular votes. Landon and the Republicans won the 8 electoral votes of Maine and Vermont and about 16,684,000 popular votes. *See also* ELECTION OF 1928 (HOOVER); ELECTION OF 1932 (FRANKLIN D. ROOSEVELT); ELECTION OF 1940 (FRANKLIN D. ROOSEVELT); ELECTION OF 1944 (FRANKLIN D. ROOSEVELT).

Election of 1940

✪ In 1940, Franklin D. Roosevelt broke the two-term tradition started by George Washington. Roosevelt won an easy victory over Republican Wendell Willkie.

▲ Roosevelt remained popular throughout his terms as president.

The Candidates In September 1939 World War II broke out in Europe. President Roosevelt declared that the United States would remain **neutral** in the conflict. But as the threat of war increased, many Americans wanted Roosevelt to run for a third term—something no other president had ever done. Before the war, Roosevelt probably did not plan to run again. After Hitler had invaded the Netherlands, Belgium, and France, however, he changed his mind. Roosevelt was also still very popular and was likely to win against a Republican nominee. By the time the **Democratic** convention met in Chicago, about three-fifths of the delegates were pledged to the president. Roosevelt easily won on the first **ballot**. For vice president, Roosevelt insisted that Secretary of Agriculture Henry A. Wallace be the nominee. Many delegates opposed Wallace, because he was seen as too **liberal**, but Roosevelt refused to run if Wallace was not on the **ticket**. Roosevelt had his way.

Several **Republicans** wanted their party's presidential nomination. The chief contenders were New York State District Attorney Thomas E. Dewey; Ohio senator Robert A. Taft, the son of former president William Howard Taft; Wendell Willkie, a New York lawyer and financial executive; and Michigan senator Arthur H. Vandenberg. When the Republican convention met in Philadelphia, the delegates became **deadlocked**, with Dewey in the lead,

> - "No Franklin
> - the First!"
> - —Anti-Roosevelt slogan, 1940

Taft in second place, Willkie third, and Vandenberg last. By the fourth ballot, Willkie was in the lead, but still failed to receive a majority of the delegates' votes. Finally, on the sixth ballot, Willkie gained the nomination. For vice president, Willkie chose Oregon senator Charles L. McNary.

The Issues The war in Europe and the third term were the two main issues of the campaign. Willkie attacked Roosevelt for breaking the two-term tradition started by George Washington, claiming that Roosevelt would ultimately become a dictator. He took a strong stand against Hitler and favored the **draft**, or forced military service, that had gone into effect in August 1940. Roosevelt promised to keep the United States out of the war. He blamed congressional Republicans for failing to keep the nation's military strong. But he said nothing about his running for a third term.

The Campaign Confident of victory, Roosevelt spent most of the campaign in Washington. In the last two weeks of the campaign, he made a series of speeches pledging to keep America out of the war and speaking out against the Republicans in Congress. Willkie traveled throughout 34 states and made more than

Henry A. Wallace (1888–1965) was born into a farming family in Iowa. His Republican father published a farming magazine and served as secretary of agriculture in the Harding and Coolidge administrations. Wallace left the Republicans in the late 1920s because he believed that the high **tariffs** favored by the party hurt farmers. In 1933, President Roosevelt appointed Wallace secretary of agriculture. Wallace worked hard to improve the lot of farmers during the Great Depression. In 1940, Roosevelt insisted that Wallace become his running mate. An energetic vice president, Wallace traveled to many countries and favored an active foreign policy. Many Democratic leaders thought that Wallace was too liberal, so when Roosevelt was planning to run for his fourth term in 1944, they convinced him to drop Wallace from the ticket. Roosevelt then made him secretary of commerce. Wallace held this position until 1946, when President Truman fired him because of policy disagreements. In 1947, Wallace announced that he was going to run for president—on the **Progressive party** ticket. He lost the election, winning a mere 2 percent of the popular vote. He then retired to his farm in New York.

World War II broke out in Europe in September 1939, when Hitler's Nazi Germany invaded Poland. By early 1940, Germany and Italy had conquered most of Europe. Only Great Britain and the Soviet Union stood against them. In the 1930s, Japan had begun expanding its empire in Asia and in the Pacific. The Japanese, who had allied with Germany and Italy, suddenly attacked the U.S. naval base at Pearl Harbor in Hawaii on December 7, 1941. The attack sank or damaged 21 ships, including 8 battleships, 3 cruisers, 4 destroyers, and 6 other vessels. The attack also destroyed 188 airplanes and killed 2,403 Americans. Another 1,178 were injured. The next day, President Roosevelt asked Congress for a declaration of war against Japan. In response, Germany and Italy declared war on the United States. War raged in Europe and in the Pacific. Italy surrendered in 1943, but Nazi Germany fought until May 1945. Japan finally surrendered in August 1945, after the United States dropped atomic bombs on the cities of Hiroshima and Nagasaki.

500 speeches trying to rally voters' support. But Willkie could not convince voters to dump the **incumbent**.

The Election On Election Day, Roosevelt won another outstanding victory, with 449 **electoral votes** to Willkie's 82. Roosevelt won about 55 percent of the popular vote to about 45 percent for Willkie. *See also* ELECTION OF 1932 (FRANKLIN D. ROOSEVELT); ELECTION OF 1936 (FRANKLIN D. ROOSEVELT); ELECTION OF 1944 (FRANKLIN D. ROOSEVELT).

Election of 1944

The Candidates By 1944, the end of World War II was in sight. As the election of 1944 approached, many people wondered if the president would run again. A week before the **Democratic** convention met, Roosevelt sent a letter to the convention chair stating that if the convention nominated him, "I shall accept. If the people elect me, I will serve. . . ." When the delegates assembled, they nominated Roosevelt on the first **ballot**. However, many delegates were opposed to placing Vice President Henry A. Wallace on the **ticket** for a second term; they viewed him as too **liberal**. Party leaders supported Missouri senator Harry S. Truman. Roosevelt agreed, and Truman received the nomination on the second ballot.

Two **Republican** leaders wanted the presidential nomination—New York governor Thomas E. Dewey and Wendell Willkie, the candidate in the ELECTION OF 1940. As the two

▲ Roosevelt served almost 13 years as president—longer than anyone else.

> • • • • • • • •
> **"Don't Change Horses in Midstream."**
> —Democratic campaign slogan, 1944

One of the most memorable stories from the 1944 campaign included President Roosevelt's dog, Fala. During a speech in September, the president noted, "These Republican leaders have not been content with attacks on me, or my wife, or my sons—they now include my little dog, Fala. Unlike members of my family, he resents this. Being a Scottie, as soon as he learned that the Republican fiction writers had concocted a story that I had left him on an Aleutian island and had sent a destroyer back to find him at a cost to the taxpayers of two or three or twenty million dollars, his Scotch soul was furious. He has not been the same since." The audience roared with approval.

Republicans squared off in the **primary elections**, it quickly became clear that Dewey was the party favorite. Thus, when the Republican convention gathered, Dewey won the nomination on the first ballot. For vice president, the Republicans chose Ohio governor John W. Bricker.

The Issues There was little difference in the views of the two parties. Dewey and the Republicans did not condemn Roosevelt's war policies. Instead they cited Roosevelt's apparently poor health and criticized the "tired old men" who had been in charge of the government for the past 12 years. In turn, the Democrats defended Roosevelt's health, calling upon his personal doctor to come to his defense: "He's perfectly O.K. . . . The stories that he is in bad health are understand-

Thomas E. Dewey (1902–1971) was a well-known lawyer and Republican political leader. After graduating from Columbia Law School, he served as United States Attorney for southern New York State. He was elected governor of New York in 1942, and won reelection in 1946 and 1950. During his time as governor, he efficiently ran the state as if it were a business. He unsuccessfully ran for president in 1944 against Franklin D. Roosevelt and again in 1948, this time against Harry S. Truman. Dewey continued to be active in politics, serving as an advisor to later Republican presidents.

able enough around election time, but they are not true."

The Campaign Dewey and the Republicans promised to build on most New Deal programs, but claimed that Roosevelt and the Democrats were wasting money. Dewey pledged to carry out government programs more efficiently. Dewey also refused to criticize the president's war policies, noting, "The military conduct of the war is outside this campaign. It is and must remain completely out of politics."

During much of the campaign, Roosevelt stayed in the White House and managed governmental business. He started giving campaign speeches in September, blasting the Republicans as being against workers and in favor of big business. The Democrats also pointed out Dewey's lack of foreign-policy experience.

The Election The voters once again put their confidence in Roosevelt and elected him to an unprecedented fourth term. Roosevelt won 432 **electoral votes** and just more than 53 percent of the popular vote. Dewey won 99 electoral votes and about 46 percent of the popular vote.

In April 1945, the president went to Warm Springs, Georgia, to relax and to prepare for the upcoming San Francisco Conference, where world leaders were to organize the United Nations (UN). On April 12, while working at his desk, he raised his hand to his forehead and said, "I have a terrible headache." He slumped into unconsciousness and died soon afterward.

Vice President Truman was called to the White House, where Mrs. Roosevelt met him with the words, "Harry, the president is dead." Stunned, Truman was at first silent, but then responded, "Is there anything I can do for you?" Calmly, Mrs. Roosevelt responded, "Is there anything we can do for you? For you are the one in trouble now." Harry S. Truman was sworn in as the thirty-third president at about 7:08 P.M. that evening. *See also* ELECTION OF 1932 (FRANKLIN D. ROOSEVELT); ELECTION OF 1936 (FRANKLIN D. ROOSEVELT); ELECTION OF 1940 (FRANKLIN D. ROOSEVELT); ELECTION OF 1948 (TRUMAN).

Election of 1948

The Candidates As the election of 1948 approached, **incumbent** Harry S. Truman planned to run for the presidency in his own right. He had assumed the presidency after the death of Franklin D. Roosevelt in 1945. Truman oversaw the end of World War II and worked to restore the nation to a peacetime economy. Yet many members of his own party criticized him—liberal **Democrats** for his strong opposition to the Soviet Union and conservative Democrats for his stand favoring civil rights. Many Democrats believed Truman could not win the presidential election and looked for another nominee. As the convention approached, some party leaders worked behind the scenes to prevent Truman's candidacy. They were unsuccessful and Truman was nominated on the first **ballot**. For vice president, the Democrats chose Kentucky senator Alben W. Barkley.

Unhappy with Truman and the Democratic **platform**, the **liberal** Democrats, calling themselves **Progressives**, held their own conven-

> ● "Give 'em hell, Harry!"
>
> —Crowds' response to Truman's criticism of the Republicans, 1948

▲ Truman won the presidency in 1948 in his own right after a rough campaign.

tion. They nominated former vice president Henry A. Wallace for president and Idaho senator Glen Taylor for vice president. The Southern conservatives, too, split from the party and held their own convention. Opposing the Democrats' stand favoring civil rights for African Americans, they nominated South Carolina senator J. Strom Thurmond for president and Mississippi governor Fielding Wright for vice president. Calling themselves the **Dixiecrats**, they opposed **integration** and hoped to throw the election into the House of Representatives.

Several **Republican** leaders wanted the presidential nomination in 1948, but Thomas E. Dewey, who had run against Roosevelt in the ELECTION OF 1944, was the party favorite. He was nominated unanimously on the third ballot. For vice president, the Republicans chose California governor Earl Warren.

Election of 1948

Candidate (Party)	Popular Vote	Electoral Vote
Harry S. Truman (Democrat)	24,179,345	303
Thomas E. Dewey (Republican)	21,991,291	189
J. Strom Thurmond (Dixiecrat)	1,176,125	39
Henry A. Wallace (Progressive)	1,157,326	0

Truman displays a newspaper headline that wrongly projected Dewey as the winner.

The Issues

Several issues confronted the nation in 1948. The Democrats favored civil rights for African Americans, better labor conditions, and national health insurance. They wanted to expand New Deal programs, such as Social Security. For the most part, the Republicans opposed moving too quickly on civil rights issues, were against national health insurance, and did not want to expand New Deal programs. They claimed they could provide the same programs more efficiently.

The Campaign

The 1948 campaign was one of the most spirited in the nation's history. The media, many voters, and even many Democrats believed Truman was doomed to lose. Truman himself, however, was confident of victory. Traveling by rail, he began a 30,000-mile whistle-stop campaign, during which he gave more than 300 speeches from the back of the train after it pulled into a station. He addressed the voters in plain language, attacking the

Republican-controlled Congress, which he called the "Do-Nothing Eightieth Congress." He pointed out that the Republicans in Congress failed to do anything about high prices and affordable housing. He also warned that the Republicans wanted to destroy the New Deal. At one campaign stop, someone from the audience yelled "Give 'em hell, Harry!" The president replied that he never deliberately gave anyone hell. He just told the truth, and they thought it was hell.

Confident of victory, Dewey generally ignored Truman. In his speeches, he avoided the issues and tried instead to convince voters that he was a public-spirited and able administrator. He promised to bring unity and effectiveness to the government. Dewey's speeches were designed to make the people feel good. In one

Elizabeth "Bess" Truman (1885–1982) was born into a prominent family in Independence, Missouri. A good student, Bess was also athletic—enjoying baseball, tennis, basketball, and fencing. Bess had known Harry Truman since childhood, but their relationship developed slowly. They married in 1919 after he returned home from World War I. Bess believed that publicity was unbecoming, so despite Harry's public career, she generally stayed in the background. Nonetheless she was a partner to her husband, reviewing his speeches and letters and helping him control his hot temper. As First Lady, she oversaw the repair of the White House. True to herself, she remained private, refusing to meet with the press or to take stands on the issues of the day. In 1953, the Trumans retired to Independence, Missouri. Bess died at age 97, about ten years after her husband.

speech, he noted, "Ours is a magnificent land. Every part of it. Don't let anyone frighten you or try to stampede you into believing that America is finished. America's future . . . is still ahead of us."

Truman continued his attacks on Dewey and the Republicans. He claimed that the Republican Congress had "cheated the people" and blamed the Republican party for the Great Depression. In early November, Truman commented on the Republican candidate's stand, "The campaign is ending and you still don't know. All you have got is platitudes and double-talk."

Wallace, the Progressive candidate, campaigned mostly in the Midwest. He claimed that the Communist Soviet Union was no threat to the United States, a stand that was becoming increasingly unpopular. When he spoke in the South, he was pelted with eggs and tomatoes. By the end of the campaign, the Progressive movement was near collapse.

Dixiecrat Strom Thurmond campaigned little and his support was mostly in the South. The Dixiecrats opposed civil rights, the elimination of **segregation**, and federal laws concerning voting and employment rights.

As Election Day drew near, the **polls** predicted a Dewey landslide. *Life* magazine's cover showed a picture of Dewey with the caption, "The next president of the United States." A nationwide newsletter predicted, "Dewey will be in for eight years—until '57." The *New York Times* claimed that Dewey would win 345 electoral votes to Truman's 105. The Chicago *Tribune* the morning after the election proclaimed "Dewey Defeats Truman." All were wrong.

The Election Despite polls that predicted a Dewey landslide, Truman and the Democrats swept to victory. Truman won 303 **electoral votes** to Dewey's 189 and Thurmond's 39. The Democrats had now won five elections in a row. Even the split in the Democratic party failed to produce the expected Republican victory. What had happened? How could the polls be so wrong? Immediately after the election, the media tried to explain their mistake. Some media experts blamed themselves for relying on the polls, without checking their facts. The press believed the pollsters' statistics without carefully considering the voters' views and feelings. Many in the press held that, with the Democratic party divided, a Republican victory was certain—just as Woodrow Wilson had won with the Republicans divided in the ELECTION OF 1912.

Dewey blamed his loss on too great a reliance on the polls, claiming that two or three million Republican voters stayed home. Most observers, however, agreed that Truman won because his campaign appealed to the people. He won the votes of workers and farmers, two important voting groups who had greatly benefited from the **Democratic party's** New Deal programs. Truman promised to expand Roosevelt's policies. The voters rejected the Republican view of the federal government's role, which had greatly changed since 1928 when Herbert Hoover was elected. *See also* ELECTION OF 1944 (FRANKLIN D. ROOSEVELT); ELECTION OF 1952 (EISENHOWER).

Election of 1952

Dwight D. Eisenhower ✪ Eisenhower was the first Republican elected to the presidency since Herbert Hoover in 1928.

The Candidates As the election of 1952 approached, most people believed that **incumbent** President Harry S. Truman would run for reelection. However, Truman surprised his party and the public when he announced that he would not seek another term. This made the **Democratic** nomination wide open—for there was no **front-runner**.

Three contenders soon emerged—Illinois

- "I Like Ike."
- —Republican campaign slogan, 1952

▲ The thirty-fourth president had served as supreme commander of the Allied forces in Western Europe in World War II.

governor Adlai Stevenson, Tennessee senator Estes Kefauver, and Senator Richard Russell of Georgia. At the Democratic convention in Chicago, Stevenson received the nomination on the third **ballot**. Stevenson, whose grandfather of the same name had served as vice president under Grover Cleveland (1893–1897), was an eloquent and witty public speaker. The convention nominated Alabama senator John J. Sparkman for vice president.

During the campaign, vice-presidential candidate Richard M. Nixon was accused of having a secret "extra expense" fund of about $18,000, given to him by rich business leaders. The accusation hurt the Republicans and almost forced Nixon off the **ticket**. To defend himself, Nixon made a televised address. He claimed to have done nothing wrong and spoke of his wife and two young daughters. But he admitted to receiving one gift from a supporter—a cocker spaniel, which his six-year-old daughter, Tricia, had named "Checkers." Near the end of the speech, Nixon said, "And you know, the kids, like all kids, love the dog; and I just want to say this right now, that regardless of what they say about it, we are going to keep him." The address, known as the "Checkers speech," helped sway the people's sympathy, and Nixon stayed on

Republican presidents are celebrated on this souvenir handkerchief from 1952.

This campaign button clearly states the voters' choice.

When the **Republican** convention met in Chicago, two strong candidates sought the nomination—General Dwight Eisenhower and Ohio senator Robert Taft, the son of former president William Howard Taft (1909–1913). The delegates' support for the two men was closely divided, but Eisenhower was nominated on the first ballot. The Republican nominee had become a popular hero to Americans during World War II.

For vice president, Eisenhower chose California senator Richard M. Nixon. Nixon was a well-known foe of Communism.

The Issues Three issues dominated the campaign—Korea, Communism, and corruption. The Korean War (1951–1953) had begun when troops from Communist North Korea invaded democratic South Korea. Yet Americans wanted the war to end quickly. The fear of Communism was widespread, especially after many eastern European countries and China fell to the Communists in the late 1940s. Accusations of corruption, the third major campaign issue, weighed down both parties.

The Campaign Eisenhower and Stevenson both campaigned extensively, traveling across the country. Eisenhower even campaigned in the South, something no Republican candidate had done in modern times. Concerning government corruption, he claimed that "The Washington mess is not a one-agency mess, or a one-bureau mess, or a one-department mess. It is a top-to-bottom mess."

Stevenson, too, spoke out against corruption. He called for better benefits and health

Mamie Eisenhower (1896–1979) was born in Iowa, but grew up in Colorado. Later, the family built a winter home in San Antonio, Texas. There, in 1915, she met her future husband, Dwight Eisenhower, who was assigned to a nearby army base. They married less than a year later. Because soldiers are frequently reassigned, Mamie was a veteran at moving—28 times! When the Eisenhowers moved into the White House, Mamie quickly took charge and, in military fashion, checked for dust wearing white gloves. She died in 1979 and is buried next to her husband in Abilene, Kansas.

care for workers, and he criticized the Republicans for stirring up the fear of Communism. Concerning the Korean War, he warned of "a long, patient, costly struggle which alone can assure triumph over the great enemies of man—war, poverty, and tyranny."

The first presidential television ad campaign was created for Eisenhower. The "Eisenhower Answers America" campaign ads, a series of short commercials, showed Eisenhower responding to voters' questions.

Speaking in Detroit in October 1952, Eisenhower promised to end the war if elected. In his speech he promised, "I shall go to Korea." The address impressed the country and Eisenhower's victory was almost assured.

The Election Almost 62 percent of eligible voters went to the polls in 1952. Eisenhower won by a landslide with 442 **electoral votes** over Stevenson's 89. *See also* ELECTION OF 1948 (TRUMAN); ELECTION OF 1956 (EISENHOWER); ELECTION OF 1960 (KENNEDY); ELECTION OF 1968 (NIXON); ELECTION OF 1972 (NIXON).

Election of 1956

Dwight D. Eisenhower ✪ Worried by threats of war, voters kept President Dwight Eisenhower in the White House.

The Candidates President Eisenhower had had a heart attack in September 1955, when he was almost 65 years old. Many Americans wondered if he would run for reelection. Eisenhower was popular with voters, the nation was at peace, the economy was strong, and the **Republican party** needed him as their leader. The president's health improved, and in February 1956, he announced his candidacy. At the Republican convention, he was nominated on the first **ballot**. Vice President Richard M. Nixon was again his running mate.

Adlai E. Stevenson, the **Democratic** nominee in 1952, announced in late 1955 that he would again seek the presidency. Within his party, he was challenged by Tennessee senator Estes Kefauver. Stevenson and Kefauver battled for the nomination in several **primary elections**, until Stevenson won a clear victory in the California primary. The Democratic convention nominated him on the first ballot. Stevenson then surprised the convention by throwing the

> ● ● ● ● ● ● ● ● ● ●
> **"The only way to win World War III is to prevent it."**
> —*President Eisenhower, radio and television address, September 19, 1956*

▲ Eisenhower won an even larger election victory than in 1952.

vice-presidential choice open, thus allowing the delegates to select his running mate. A struggle began between Massachusetts senator John F. Kennedy and Kefauver. In a close contest, Kefauver won second place on the **ticket**.

The Issues The 1956 campaign focused on Eisenhower's health, national defense, and foreign policy. The parties differed on the best way to maintain world peace and on how to deal with the Communist-ruled nations, especially the Soviet Union and China. The parties also presented different views about nuclear weapons and their testing.

The Campaign To help put aside questions about his health, Eisenhower personally campaigned in 13 states, covering about 14,000 miles. Vice President Nixon traveled throughout the country for the Republican ticket, attacking Stevenson as inexperienced in foreign policy.

In 1954, the United States Supreme Court decided in *Brown v. Board of Education of Topeka, Kansas*, that segregated public schools violated the civil rights of minorities. This decision, and the effort to integrate public schools, began a new civil rights movement. Throughout 1955 and the election year of 1956, civil rights activists struggled against terrible and sometimes violent opposition. During the 1956 campaign, however, neither Eisenhower nor Stevenson expressed open support for racial integration. They believed that doing so would have cost them too many votes.

Senator Estes Kefauver (1903–1963) of Tennessee was known for his folksy manner and keen mind. He campaigned for the Democratic presidential nomination in 1952 and 1956, even though the leaders of the Democratic party favored Adlai Stevenson. In 1956, Kefauver stunned the Democrats by winning the New Hampshire primary election with 84 percent of the vote. Although Stevenson received the nomination, Kefauver's successes in the primaries made him the party's choice for vice president. After 1956, candidates followed Kefauver's example and worked harder to win the primary elections.

On the other hand, Stevenson traveled more than 37,000 miles in an effort to reach the voters. He raised questions about the president's health, claiming that Vice President Nixon would assume the presidency within the next four years. He called for an end to the testing of nuclear weapons. Stevenson claimed that the United States was militarily unprepared and wanted to end the draft—the calling of young men to serve in the nation's army. He planned to replace the draft with a specially trained all-volunteer army.

In the months before the election, two serious international events occurred. Israel, France, and Great Britain attacked Egypt in response to that nation's taking over the Suez Canal. And in October 1956, the Soviet army invaded Hungary to stop a revolt against Communist rule. American voters watched these events uneasily. On Election Day, most people decided they wanted a strong military and a president who could keep the United States out of war.

The Election President Eisenhower won reelection by a landslide, winning more than 35,000,000 popular votes to Stevenson's 26,000,000. In the **Electoral College**, the Republican margin of victory was 457 to 73. *See also* ELECTION OF 1952 (EISENHOWER); ELECTION OF 1960 (KENNEDY).

The Candidates As the 1960 election neared, Vice President Richard Nixon was the **Republican party's** favorite. Nixon, who had served in the House of Representatives and the Senate before becoming vice president, was well known across the nation. He had made headlines in 1948 as the head of a House subcommittee that investigated Alger Hiss, a State Department employee suspected of being a Soviet spy. For vice president, the Republicans chose former Massachusetts senator Henry Cabot Lodge.

Several men sought the **Democratic** nomination. Among them were Missouri senator Stuart Symington, Minnesota senator Hubert H. Humphrey, Texas senator Lyndon B. Johnson, former candidate Adlai E. Stevenson, and Massachusetts senator John F. Kennedy. Humphrey and Kennedy entered several of the Democratic **primary elections** to demonstrate their voter appeal. The other candidates planned to gain support from party leaders at the convention.

Many Americans questioned Kennedy's candidacy because of his Roman Catholic religion. The test of whether voters would support a Catholic candidate came in West Virginia, a state that was 95 percent Protestant. Humphrey and Kennedy squared off in the state's primary. Kennedy won an outstanding primary victory, capturing all but 7 of the state's 55 counties.

> ● ● ● ● ● ● ● ● ● ● ● ● ●
> **"We stand today on the edge of a New Frontier— the frontier of the 1960s. . . ."**
> —*John F. Kennedy, nomination acceptance speech, 1960*

▲ The thirty-fifth president, at 43 years of age, was the youngest man to be elected president.

Humphrey was forced to end his candidacy. Kennedy then went on to win all the remaining primaries, assuring his nomination at the Democratic convention. For vice president, Kennedy selected Lyndon B. Johnson of Texas, a former rival for the nomination. This choice strengthened the Democrats' Southern support.

Kennedy came from a wealthy and prominent Boston family. A World War II hero, he was elected to the House in 1946 and the Senate in 1952. Kennedy was also the author of two best-selling nonfiction books: *Why England Slept*, about Great Britain before World War II, and *Profiles in Courage*, which won a Pulitzer Prize in 1957.

The Issues The two main issues in 1960 were the nation's economy and the threat of Communism. Kennedy and the Democrats blamed the Republicans for the economic **recession** that had hit the nation in the late 1950s. To highlight Kennedy's youth and relative inexperience, the Republicans pointed to Nixon's foreign-policy knowledge. They noted that it was key to fighting the Communist threat. For some voters, Kennedy's Roman Catholic faith remained an issue. In this campaign, the issues were less important than the appeal of the candidates themselves.

The Campaign The candidates and their supporters waged an aggressive campaign, crossing the country trying to sway the voters. The Republicans stressed Nixon's experience as the most active vice president in history. But this campaign tactic came under question when a reporter asked President Eisenhower for an example of a decision in which Nixon had taken part. Eisenhower replied, "If you give me a week, I might think of one." Some suggested Eisenhower was trying to make a joke about his own bad memory. But to many people, it seemed he was saying Nixon was not important in the administration.

"Let's get America moving again" became the theme of Kennedy's campaign. He thus called attention to the poor economy and, indirectly, to the age of President Eisenhower and many of his advisers. Nixon forbade his campaign staff to raise the issue of Kennedy's religion. But some Protestant clergy questioned whether Kennedy would be able to separate his allegiance to the pope in Rome from his duties as president. He confronted this issue in a speech in Houston, saying "I believe in an America where separation of Church and State is absolute, where no Catholic prelate would tell the President (should he be Catholic)

Jacqueline Bouvier Kennedy (1929–1994) grew up in a wealthy family and attended private schools. In 1951, she graduated with an art degree from George Washington University. She met Senator John F. Kennedy in 1951 and they married two years later. Jacqueline, or "Jackie," became First Lady when she was only 31 years old, bringing grace, charm, and youth to the White House. She renovated the White House and made it a center for culture and the arts. In 1962, she led a televised tour of the redecorated White House, which increased her popularity. But Jackie tried to maintain the family's privacy, especially for the Kennedys' two small children, Caroline and John.

Jackie was in the car sitting next to her husband when he was struck by an assassin's bullet on November 22, 1963. That same day, still wearing a pink dress stained with her husband's blood, she stood by Lyndon B. Johnson while he was sworn in as the next president. She died in 1994 and is buried next to her husband in Arlington National Cemetery in Virginia.

how to act and no Protestant minister would tell his parishioners for whom to vote."

The first televised debates in presidential campaign history occurred during the 1960 campaign. Nixon and Kennedy spoke in four live debates that were watched by six million voters on national television. The debates revealed the power of television as a campaign tool.

Nixon went into the debates with confidence. His past television appearances, such as the "Checkers speech" (*see* ELECTION OF 1952) had been good for his career. Nixon believed that he could impress viewers with his superior experience.

During the first debate, however, Nixon did not look confident. He felt pain from an injured knee, and he was tired from hard campaigning. He had lost weight, and his clothes did not fit well. He looked pale and sweated heavily. Kennedy had also been campaigning and preparing for the debates, but he looked rested and tanned. He appeared handsome, youthful, and energetic, and he soon put Nixon on the defensive.

The way the candidates looked had a bigger impact on the television audience than what they said. After the debate ended, most television viewers said Kennedy had won. A majority of those who listened on the radio believed that Nixon had won. The three following debates had similar outcomes.

Kennedy and the Democrats also reached out to African Americans and other minority voters. For example, in October 1960, Dr. Martin Luther King, Jr., was arrested at a civil rights demonstration. Kennedy called Dr. King's wife, Coretta Scott King, and expressed concern. This won Kennedy the support of many African American voters. Vice-presidential candidate Lyndon B. Johnson helped sway Hispanic voters in Texas.

The Election The election of 1960 was one of the closest in the nation's history. The outcome of the election was uncertain until early the next morning. Kennedy had won the popular vote by 34,226,731 to 34,108,157—a difference of only 118,574 votes nationwide. In the **Electoral College**, the vote was 303 to 219.

The popular vote was unbelievably close. A shift of just a few thousand votes in three tight states—Missouri (4,991 votes), Illinois (4,430 votes), and New Jersey (11,046 votes)—would have given Nixon an Electoral College victory, even though he would still have lost the popular vote. Those 20,467 popular votes represent only 0.03 percent of the national total.

Sadly, President Kennedy was assassinated while riding in a motorcade in Dallas, Texas, on November 22, 1963. Vice President Lyndon B. Johnson was sworn in as the thirty-sixth president. *See also* ELECTION OF 1952 (EISENHOWER); ELECTION OF 1956 (EISENHOWER); ELECTION OF 1964 (LYNDON JOHNSON).

The Election of 1960

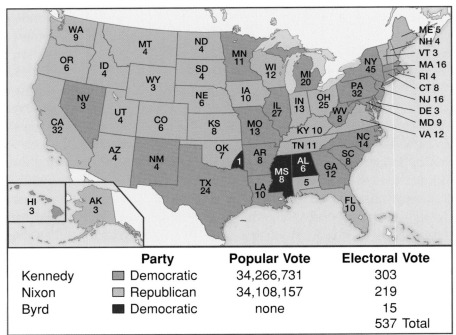

	Party	Popular Vote	Electoral Vote
Kennedy	■ Democratic	34,266,731	303
Nixon	☐ Republican	34,108,157	219
Byrd	■ Democratic	none	15
			537 Total

The election of 1960 was one of the closest in the nation's history. Senator Harry F. Byrd of Virginia, who did not campaign, received 15 electoral votes.

Election of 1964

Lyndon B. Johnson ✪ Johnson easily won election to a term of his own in 1964.

▲ The thirty-sixth president won office in one of the greatest landslides in election history.

The Candidates Vice President Lyndon B. Johnson had assumed the presidency on November 22, 1963, after the assassination of President Kennedy. As president, Johnson worked hard to enact many of Kennedy's programs. With the election of 1964 approaching, it was clear that Johnson would be the **Democratic** nominee.

Texan Lyndon Johnson had been elected to the United States House of Representatives in 1937 and to the Senate in 1948. By 1955, he was Senate majority leader, and he became vice president in the ELECTION OF 1960. Johnson easily won the Democratic nomination in 1964. For vice president, Johnson chose liberal Minnesota senator Hubert H. Humphrey.

At first, no clear nominee emerged in the **Republican party**, but the two leading contenders were conservative Arizona senator Barry Goldwater and moderate governor Nelson Rockefeller of New York. Goldwater scored key victories in the **primary elections**, and after a divisive convention, won the Republican nomination on the first **ballot**. For his running mate, Goldwater chose upstate New York representative William G. Miller, although he had few qualifications for high office.

Goldwater was a former business executive who had served in the Senate since 1952. In his acceptance speech, the conservative Goldwater told the Republicans, "I would remind you that extremism in the defense of liberty is no vice. And let me remind you also that moderation in the pursuit of justice is no virtue."

> - "All the way with L.B.J."
> —Democratic campaign slogan, 1964

Lady Bird Johnson (1912–) was born into a successful farm family in Texas. Her given name was Claudia Alta Taylor, but a nanny gave her the nickname "Lady Bird" as a baby. Lady Bird graduated from high school at age 15. She went to the University of Texas, graduating with degrees in journalism and liberal arts. She met her future husband, Lyndon B. Johnson, in 1934, and they married only two months later. In 1942, Lady Bird bought a Texas radio station, which she expanded into a multimillion-dollar business. Lady Bird was an active First Lady and campaigned for her husband during the 1964 campaign, especially through the South. After Lyndon was elected, she worked with Congress to pass the Highway Beautification Act of 1965, which led to the planting of flowers and trees along the nation's roadways. After President Johnson chose not to run for reelection in 1968, the couple retired to their ranch in Texas.

War had raged in Vietnam since the end of World War II in 1945. The United States worried that the Vietnamese Communists, who controlled the northern part of the country, would gain complete control. Presidents Truman, Eisenhower, and Kennedy had sent advisors and large amounts of financial aid to South Vietnam. But the South Vietnamese governments were weak and corrupt, and the Communists continued to gain support.

By 1964, a new South Vietnamese government was in danger of falling to the Communists. President Johnson, not wanting Vietnam to fall to the Communists while he was running for election, tried to strengthen that nation's military. In August 1964, North Vietnam allegedly attacked an American destroyer in the waters off the North Vietnamese coast. In response, Congress passed the Gulf of Tonkin Resolution, which authorized Johnson to "take all necessary measures to repel any armed attack against the forces of the United States." Johnson then authorized limited bombing raids, beginning in 1965. The nation's role in the war continued to grow until about 500,000 American troops were in Vietnam. A treaty restoring peace to Vietnam was finally signed in January 1973.

Johnson's 1964 campaign emphasized rights for women and minorities.

The Issues The major issue of the campaign was America's role in the Vietnam War (1954–1973). Johnson called for a limited American role, while Goldwater favored the use of nuclear weapons if necessary. In addition, Johnson planned to expand the social programs of Roosevelt's New Deal (*see* ELECTION OF 1932). In contrast, Goldwater wanted to dismantle these programs, calling for an end to Social Security and all farm aid.

The Campaign At the start of the campaign, Goldwater promised Americans "a choice, not an echo." Indeed, many of his very conserva-

During the 1964 campaign, Lyndon Johnson promised to expand the government's social policies, which had been in place since Franklin D. Roosevelt's administrations (1933–1945). After winning a landslide victory in the 1964 election, Johnson expanded New Deal programs with his Great Society. The Great Society centered on five key areas: the war on poverty, increased civil rights, Medicare and Medicaid, environmental protections, and consumer safety.

Johnson launched his Great Society soon after his inauguration. The Job Corps, VISTA, Head Start, and other programs were designed to fight the war on poverty. Three major laws expanded civil rights. The Civil Rights Act of 1964 barred discrimination in employment, as well as in hotels, restaurants, and other public places. The Voting Rights Act of 1965 protected the rights of African American voters in the South. The Civil Rights Act of 1968 banned discrimination in the sale and rental of housing. Medicare provided hospital insurance and some medical coverage to people older than age 65. Medicaid offered hospital and medical benefits to the poor.

To protect the environment, Congress passed the Water Quality Act of 1965, the Clean Air Act of 1965, and the Air Quality Act of 1967. New consumer safeguards included several laws: the Fair Packaging and Labeling Act of 1966, the National Traffic Safety Act of 1966, the Highway Safety Act of 1966, and the Wholesome Meat Act of 1968.

tive proposals were far from the nations' beliefs. For example, his suggestion that Social Security be made voluntary frightened senior citizens. His opposition to most civil rights laws turned away African Americans and other minorities. And his call for nuclear weapons in Vietnam frightened much of the nation.

Democrats used Goldwater's ideas to portray him as dangerous. On domestic issues, the Democrats said Senator Goldwater was out of step with the nation because he voted against most civil rights laws and a nuclear test-ban treaty. Concerning Vietnam, the Democrats held that Goldwater would start a nuclear war. One especially effective Johnson television ad showed a peaceful scene with a young girl counting daisy petals. The scene suddenly changed to a rising nuclear mushroom cloud, with a man's voice counting down the detonation of an atomic bomb. The ad aired only once, but clearly labeled Goldwater as the candidate who favored nuclear war.

In the meantime, Johnson assured voters that he would not send troops to Vietnam. In a speech in Akron, Ohio, he said, "We are not about to send American boys nine or ten thousand miles away from home to do what Asian boys ought to be doing for themselves." Johnson clearly made himself the candidate of peace.

The Election On Election Day, Johnson won the election easily, defeating Goldwater by 43,129,566 to 27,178,188 popular votes. The **Electoral College** vote was 486 for Johnson and 52 for Goldwater. Johnson swept the nation, with Goldwater carrying only his home state of Arizona and five states of the Deep South—Louisiana, Mississippi, Alabama, Georgia, and South Carolina. *See also* ELECTION OF 1960 (KENNEDY); ELECTION OF 1968 (NIXON).

Election of 1968

Richard M. Nixon ⊙ Nixon won the presidency in a hotly contested election after a campaign that was marred by violence and tragedy.

The Candidates Most people assumed that **incumbent** president Lyndon B. Johnson would run for a full second term. Early in 1968, however, other **Democrats** also sought the presidency, mainly because they opposed Johnson's stand on the Vietnam War (1954–1973). Among the challengers were Minnesota senator Eugene McCarthy and New York senator Robert F. Kennedy, the brother of the late president John F. Kennedy.

Johnson's popularity dropped as the casualties from the Vietnam War increased and the war dragged on. After polls showed that he would lose the 1968 Wisconsin **primary election** to Senator McCarthy, Johnson withdrew from the race, saying that he would not seek or accept the Democratic nomination. The president's withdrawal allowed Vice President Hubert H. Humphrey to enter the campaign.

Bloodshed stained the 1968 campaign. Senator Kennedy, the early Democratic **front-runner**, was shot and killed by an assassin just after winning the California primary. The American people, already shocked by the recent murder of civil rights leader Dr. Martin Luther King, Jr., wanted law and order restored to the nation.

Yet when the 1968 Democratic convention met in Chicago, fighting broke out between antiwar protesters and the police. Despite the lack of party unity, the convention chose Vice President Humphrey on the first **ballot**. For

> • "Nixon's the
> • One!"
> •
> • —Republican campaign
>   slogan, 1968

▲ Nixon promised to end the war in Vietnam and restore law and order at home.

second place on the **ticket**, the Democrats selected Senator Edmund S. Muskie of Maine.

In contrast, the **Republican** convention in Miami was smooth and orderly. At first three Republicans— former vice president Richard M. Nixon, New York governor Nelson Rockefeller, and Michigan governor George Romney—sought the nomination. But Nixon, who had run for president in 1960, quickly became the front-runner. He was nominated on the first ballot. For the vice-presidential nominee, the Republicans chose Maryland governor Spiro T. Agnew.

A strong third-party candidate also emerged. The **American Independent party** nominated Alabama governor George Wallace, a conservative who strongly opposed integration—the mixing of black and white Americans. For vice president, the party nominated former U.S. Air Force general Curtis LeMay.

The Issues The Vietnam War and unrest at home were the two key issues of the campaign. Throughout the campaign, each candidate offered very different views to the voters.

The Campaign Nixon was far ahead in the polls at the beginning of the campaign. To maintain this lead, he avoided specifics on the main issues, promising to restore law and order and claiming to have a secret plan to end the war. Wallace appealed to people who opposed integration and called for law and order. He called for a complete military victory in Vietnam and an end to many civil rights programs. Vice President Humphrey was unable to distance himself from President Johnson's unpopular policies on the war. He stated that he would try to honorably end the war and that he supported Johnson's social and civil rights policies. Humphrey promised to end the bombing of Vietnam if it would lead to peace talks. Despite Nixon's early lead, Humphrey was able to gain support as the election approached, especially after President Johnson completely halted the bombing of

---

Pat Nixon (1912–1993) was born in California. Her given name was Thelma Catherine Ryan, but she was called "Pat" because her birthday was March 16, the day before St. Patrick's Day. Pat entered the University of Southern California in 1932, graduated with honors, and became a teacher. She met her future husband, Richard Nixon, when they were performing together in a local theater. He proposed to her on their first date, but she refused. They finally married two years later. Pat was never happy with her husband's life in politics, preferring a more private life. But she dutifully supported her husband's career, becoming a proper political wife. After becoming First Lady in 1969, she collected more than five hundred original antiques and paintings for the White House. She also made the White House more accessible to the disabled and started seasonal garden tours for the public. After President Nixon resigned in 1974, the couple retired to their home in San Clemente, California. She died there in 1993.

North Vietnam on October 31, 1968.

The Election Voters went to the polls on November 5 to cast their ballots. The popular vote between the major candidates was close—31,785,480 for Nixon and 31,275,165 for Humphrey. Wallace received 9,906,473 votes. The **Electoral College** vote was 301 for Nixon, 197 for Humphrey, and 46 for Wallace—all from the southern states of Arkansas, Louisiana, Mississippi, Alabama, and Georgia. If Wallace's support had been greater and no candidate had received an Electoral College majority, the House of Representatives would have decided the election. *See also* ELECTION OF 1952 (EISENHOWER); ELECTION OF 1956 (EISENHOWER); ELECTION OF 1960 (KENNEDY); ELECTION OF 1964 (LYNDON B. JOHNSON); ELECTION OF 1972 (NIXON).

Election of 1972

The Candidates President Nixon was renominated on the first **ballot** at the **Republican** convention. Spiro T. Agnew was again chosen for vice president. The Republican candidates were popular among many voters, particularly older Americans. During his first term, Nixon had improved relations with the Soviet Union, and the two nations signed the Strategic Arms Limitation Treaty (SALT I), which limited nuclear weapons. The president also made a triumphant goodwill trip to China. For more than 20 years, Communist China was viewed as a menace to democracy and closed to Americans. Now Americans saw the leaders of China toasting their president and promising peaceful relations.

Several **Democrats** sought the nomination of their party. They included former vice president Hubert Humphrey, New York mayor John Lindsay, Minnesota senator Eugene McCarthy, South Dakota senator George McGovern, Maine senator Edmund Muskie, and Alabama governor George Wallace. New York

▲ Nixon resigned from the presidency in August 1974.

> ● "President
> ● Nixon. Now
> ● more than
> ● ever."
> ● —*Republican campaign button, 1972*

congresswoman Shirley Chisholm also worked for the nomination, becoming the first African American woman to seek a major party nomination.

The Democrats fought for their party's nomination in the **primary elections**. At first, Governor Wallace did well in some southern primaries, but in May he was shot in an assassination attempt and left paralyzed for the rest of his life. Soon the leading contenders were Humphrey and McGovern. By the time the Democratic Convention met in July 1972, it was clear that McGovern would win the nomination, and he was chosen on the first ballot. For vice president, McGovern chose Missouri senator Thomas Eagleton. Nineteen days later, however, Eagleton resigned from the **ticket** because the **press** reported he had received shock treatments for depression. In his place, McGovern chose Peace Corps

A silver medallion celebrated the second inauguration of President Richard M. Nixon and Vice President Spiro T. Agnew.

In the early hours of June 17, 1972, Frank Willis, a guard at the Watergate hotel and office complex, spotted a piece of tape on a door lock. He summoned District of Columbia police, who found five men crouching in the dark of the Democratic National Committee offices in the Watergate complex. The men were arrested for burglary.

Newspaper reporters quickly discovered that one of the burglars, James McCord, was an ex-CIA agent and a member of President Nixon's campaign committee, called the Committee to Reelect the President (CREEP). Soon reports surfaced that the burglars were paid to commit the break-in from a secret CREEP fund controlled by the White House.

A coverup began. Administration officials destroyed evidence linking the White House to the break-in. President Nixon stepped in and denied any knowledge of it. For a time, this strategy worked and most Americans believed the president. But after his landslide reelection, the cover-up unraveled. It came to light that CREEP had authorized the Watergate break-in to find out secret information about the Democrats' campaign plans. Furthermore, secret White House tape recordings showed that the president and his aides had conspired to obstruct justice by covering up what they knew and how they were involved. In July 1974 the House Judiciary Committee voted for the president's impeachment, charging obstruction of justice, failure to uphold the law, and refusal to produce evidence. Before the articles of impeachment could be brought to a vote before the entire House of Representatives, however, President Nixon resigned.

director Sargent Shriver, the brother-in-law of President John F. Kennedy.

The Issues The Vietnam War (1954–1973) was once again the major issue of the campaign. In four years, Richard Nixon had not ended the war, but McGovern promised to end it quickly. McGovern also claimed that the Nixon administration was corrupt. (The Watergate break-in, which would eventually cause Nixon's resignation, had occurred June 1972. Most of the facts about Watergate were known, but the administration's role in the break-in was hidden by a massive coverup.)

The Campaign President Nixon led McGovern in the **polls** throughout the campaign, so he made few personal and television appearances. Nixon's running mate, Vice President Spiro T. Agnew, campaigned for the Republican ticket and condemned anyone who criticized the president or his policies. Nixon himself remained above the **mudslinging** of campaign politics.

McGovern campaigned as a peace candidate. He promised to bring American troops home from Vietnam within 90 days after being elected. He supported a minimum annual income for every American, called for tax reform, and wanted to cut defense spending. McGovern received most of his support from younger people and his antiwar message was popular on college campuses.

Nixon's supporters criticized McGovern's ideas about the military, saying that they would leave the United States vulnerable to Soviet attack. Regarding Vietnam, they believed that Nixon's policies were bringing the war to an orderly close that would not embarrass the United States. And McGovern's annual income idea sounded like socialism to Nixon's supporters.

Nixon also was able to make the antiwar movement an issue. Many people saw the antiwar protesters as Communist sympathizers

Gerald R. Ford (1913–) became the thirty-eighth president of the United States without winning a single popular vote or Electoral College vote. He was appointed to the vice presidency in 1973 after Spiro Agnew resigned. He then became president in 1974 after Richard Nixon left the office in disgrace. Ford had been elected to the House of Representatives from Michigan in 1948 and became minority leader in 1965. During his long career in the House, Ford had earned a reputation for honesty and integrity. As vice president, he brought these two important characteristics to the scandal-ridden Nixon administration. After becoming president in 1974, Ford declared, "Our long national nightmare is over." He chose Nelson Rockefeller, a former governor of New York, as his vice president. Ford and Rockefeller are the only unelected presidential team in American history.

who wanted to destroy democracy. The Nixon campaign portrayed the antiwar protesters as anti-American. Thus many voters viewed McGovern, the antiwar candidate, as anti-American.

The Election In one of the largest election landslides in American history, Nixon won every state except Massachusetts. Nixon's popular vote was 47,169,911 to McGovern's 29,170,383. The lopsided **Electoral College** vote was 520 to 17. For the first time, citizens between the ages of 18 and 20 were able to vote for the president. The Twenty-sixth Amendment, **ratified** in 1971, lowered the legal voting age from 21 to 18.

The Nixon administration soon went from triumph to disgrace. Vice President Agnew admitted taking bribes while governor of Maryland and resigned. In his place, President Nixon appointed Gerald R. Ford as vice president, as called for by the Twenty-fifth Amendment. Then in 1974, as a result of the Watergate controversy, the House of Representatives began **impeachment** proceedings against the president. It became clear that Nixon would be impeached by the House and convicted in the Senate. On August 8, 1974, President Nixon announced that he would resign the presidency at noon the next day. Gerald R. Ford was sworn in as the thirty-eighth president. *See also* ELECTION OF 1952 (EISENHOWER); ELECTION OF 1956 (EISENHOWER); ELECTION OF 1960 (KENNEDY); ELECTION OF 1968 (NIXON); ELECTION OF 1976 (CARTER).

This 1972 campaign button stresses the importance of Nixon's presidential leadership.

Election of 1976

The Candidates As the election of 1976 approached, **incumbent** president Gerald R. Ford wanted to win the presidency in his own right. After taking over the office, he had widespread popular support. However, just a month after his swearing-in, Ford granted Nixon a full and unconditional pardon for any crimes he might have committed while in office. Many Americans were angry at this decision, but Ford defended it as necessary to help heal the nation's wounds. The president's popularity fell.

During the **primary elections**, President Ford received strong competition from the **conservative** California governor, Ronald Reagan. Ford and Reagan went to the **Republican** Convention with nearly the same number of delegate votes. Ford finally won the closely contested nomination on the first **ballot**. For vice president, Ford chose Kansas senator Robert Dole, a conservative who was acceptable to Reagan and his supporters.

After the scandals of Nixon's administration, several **Democrats** were eager to run for the presidency. Among them were Arizona representative Morris Udall, former Alabama governor George Wallace, Washington senator Henry Jackson, California governor Jerry Brown, and former Georgia governor Jimmy Carter. Carter was a **dark-horse** candidate who was not well known outside of his home state. Many people asked "Jimmy who?" The

▲ The thirty-ninth President of the United States graduated from the United States Naval Academy and owned a large peanut farm in Plains, Georgia.

> • "I will never
> • lie to you."
> —*Jimmy Carter, presidential campaign, 1976*

Democratic primaries were hotly contested, but Carter campaigned hard and won impressive victories. When the Democratic convention met in New York in June 1976, Carter had won enough delegates to secure the nomination on the first ballot. For vice president, he chose liberal Minnesota senator Walter F. Mondale.

The Issues Most Americans, after the long Vietnam War and the Watergate scandal, wanted a fresh start in government. The two candidates thus tried to focus the voters' attention on the future. Both Ford and Carter were moderates who agreed on many issues—favoring civil rights for minorities, equal rights for women, and a belief that **inflation** should be brought under control.

The Campaign Jimmy Carter ran as an "outsider" who could clean up Washington from the corruption of the past. He often promised audiences "I will never lie to you." Although Ford had not been involved in the Watergate scandals, Carter tried to show that Ford was just an extension of the Nixon administration.

Ford portrayed himself in a positive light as a strong candidate working to bring the nation together. Said President Ford, "The question in this campaign of 1976 is not who

Rosalynn Carter (1927–   ) grew up in Plains, Georgia, about three miles from the home of her future husband, Jimmy Carter. They had their first date when she was 17, and they married about a year later. After their marriage, they moved several times because of Jimmy's naval career. In 1953, they moved back to Plains so that Jimmy could take over the family peanut farm. Rosalynn actively campaigned for her husband when he was running for governor of Georgia and later for president, traveling thousands of miles giving speeches. As First Lady, Rosalynn remained busy, advising the president at home and representing him overseas. She worked for better conditions for the mentally ill and for the rights of older Americans, as well as for equality for women. Rosalynn was one of the most active First Ladies since Eleanor Roosevelt. After Jimmy lost his reelection bid in 1980, the Carters retired to their farm in Plains, where she wrote an account of her years in the White House. She became active in Habitat for Humanity and other charitable groups and supported the Carter Foundation, an organization devoted to human rights and world peace.

has the better vision of America. The question is who will act to make the vision a reality." Ford trailed badly as the campaign began. After the nominating conventions, Carter enjoyed a 30-point lead in the **polls**, but the race soon became very close.

The candidates agreed to three televised debates, the first such debates since John F. Kennedy debated Richard M. Nixon. In the first debate, neither man won a clear victory, although many television viewers believed that Ford had a slight edge.

In the second debate, President Ford made a serious mistake. He stated that there was "no Soviet domination of eastern Europe" when, in fact, the Soviet Union did exert great control over the region. Voters were shocked at this misstep. This error, replayed in news stories for several days after, damaged Ford's campaign. But in the third debate, the candidates again held their own, with neither man impressing audiences.

The Election The final polls before Election Day showed the candidates neck and neck. But on November 2, Jimmy Carter won a very close race—40,827,394 popular votes over Gerald Ford's 39,145,977. The **Electoral College** count was 297 to 240. *See also* ELECTION OF 1960 (KENNEDY); ELECTION OF 1972 (NIXON); ELECTION OF 1980 (REAGAN).

Election of 1980

Ronald W. Reagan ✪ Reagan, a former film star and president of the Screen Actors Guild, found support among both Republican and Democratic conservatives.

The Candidates President Jimmy Carter sought the **Democratic** nomination in 1980 but faced a serious challenge from Massachusetts senator Edward "Ted" Kennedy, brother of the late president John F. Kennedy. Both Carter and Kennedy campaigned hard during the **primary elections**, but Carter earned most of the delegates' votes. He won renomination on the first **ballot**. Again, his running mate was Walter Mondale.

By 1980, former California governor Ronald Reagan was the **front-runner** for the **Republican** nomination. Reagan, a former Hollywood actor, dominated the primary elections, winning victories over several contenders, including Tennessee senator Howard Baker, former Texas governor John Connally, and George H.W. Bush of Texas. At the Republican Convention in July, Reagan won the nomination on the first ballot. At the convention, there were behind-the-scenes negotiations to name former president Gerald Ford as Reagan's running mate. But Ford finally declined the offer. Instead, Reagan chose Bush, a candidate with foreign-policy experience.

Representative John B. Anderson of Illinois, a moderate Republican, ran as an independent candidate. For vice president, Anderson chose Patrick J. Lucey, a former Democratic governor of Wisconsin.

- **"Are you better off now than you were four years ago?"**
  —*Candidate Ronald Reagan, 1980*

▲ At almost 70 years of age, Ronald Reagan was the oldest president ever elected.

The Issues Two issues dominated the campaign. The first focused on America's image as a world power. The second issue was the economy.

Many people believed that America's prestige had suffered as a result of the nation's involvement in Vietnam. Then, on November 4, 1979, the nation's stature suffered another blow. Iranian revolutionaries seized the United States embassy in Tehran, Iran, holding 52 American citizens hostage. The revolutionaries, who had the support of the Iranian government, demanded that their hated former leader, the Shah of Iran, be turned over to them in exchange for the hostages. The Shah had been allowed into the United States for medical treatment.

The American public was outraged and called on the government to bring the hostages home. President Carter halted oil imports from Iran to bring pressure on the Iranian government. He also tried to reason with the Iranians through diplomatic means. These efforts had no effect, and many Americans felt that the Carter administration was not doing enough. A rescue attempt in April 1980 failed when American helicopters were damaged by a sandstorm and eight rescuers were killed. The president seemed powerless to deal with the Iranian hostage crisis.

At home, the country was suffering from **inflation**. The economy seemed out of control—prices and unemployment were rising. Foreign oil producers had raised their prices from $13 to more than $34 a barrel, which made the cost of manufacturing and shipping many products much higher. Americans found that their money bought less and less.

The Campaign

President Carter's campaign staff decided that Carter's biggest advantage was that he was the **incumbent**. They worked to create an image of the president as wise and reasonable and tried to portray Reagan as reckless and dangerous.

Yet Carter's biggest disadvantage was how the voters viewed his years as president. The major problems that faced his administration— the Iranian hostage crisis and inflation—could not be easily solved, and many people held the president responsible for them.

During the campaign, Carter usually stayed in the White House, tending to the affairs of government and trying to end the Iranian hostage crisis. Reagan campaigned aggressively. He called for more forceful action to free the hostages in Iran and for a large tax cut to stimulate the economy. He advocated increased military spending and a

Nancy Reagan (1921–   ), whose given name was Anne Frances Robbins, was adopted at age 14 and became Nancy Davis. She moved to Hollywood in 1949 to start a movie career. There she met actor Ronald Reagan, who was also president of the Screen Actors Guild at that time, and they married in 1952. When her husband entered politics, first running for governor of California and later for president, Nancy actively campaigned for him. When she first became First Lady, she was criticized for spending too much money on fashionable clothes and for redecorating the White House (even though most of the money came from private donations). Later, she became involved in the campaign against drug abuse, such as the "Just Say 'No!'" program. She also supported international antidrug efforts. Soon she was very popular. As First Lady, she had a great influence on the president, and he often consulted her on issues. After eight years in the White House, the Reagans retired to California.

stronger stand against the Soviet Union.

As in the ELECTION OF 1960 and the ELECTION OF 1976, the candidates were scheduled to appear in televised debates. However, independent John Anderson was also invited to the first debate. President Carter wanted to debate only Reagan one-on-one, so he refused to attend. This was a strategic mistake. Both Reagan and Anderson used the first debate to criticize Carter, who was not there to defend himself.

In the second debate, Carter and Reagan met without Anderson. However, President Carter was still at a disadvantage. Reagan, the former film star, displayed wit, confidence, and stage presence. Compared with Reagan, Carter seemed weak and uncertain. Reagan won the audience, and the voters.

The Election Reagan scored an election landslide. He received almost 44,000,000 popular votes to Carter's 35,400,000. The **Electoral College** vote was even more lopsided—489 to 49. Anderson received no electoral votes, but earned more than 5,000,000 popular votes. *See also* ELECTION OF 1976 (CARTER); ELECTION OF 1984 (REAGAN).

Election of 1984

Ronald W. Reagan ✪ Reagan won reelection with the largest Electoral College vote in campaign history.

The Candidates President Reagan's popularity with most Americans was high as his first term entered its final months. The economy was improving, and people were finding it easier to get jobs. Reagan was unopposed for the **Republican** nomination and the party enthusiastically renominated him. George H.W. Bush was again the Republican choice for vice president.

The **Democratic front-runner** was Walter F. Mondale, a former Minnesota senator and vice president during the Carter administration. But Colorado senator Gary Hart and the Reverend Jesse Jackson of Illinois challenged Mondale. Mondale and his supporters rallied and worked hard to win in the **primary elections**. When the Democratic Convention met in San Francisco in July, Mondale had enough delegates to win the nomination on the first **ballot**.

Mondale's bold choice for second place on the Democratic **ticket** made history. He selected Representative Geraldine Ferraro of

▲ Reagan was the first president to serve two full terms since Dwight D. Eisenhower (1953–1961).

- "**Four More Years!**"
- *—Republican campaign button, 1984*

New York as his vice-presidential running mate. Ferraro was the first woman on a major party's presidential ticket. She was popular with both conservative and liberal voters in her district, and the Democrats hoped she would attract more voters, especially women, to the ticket.

The Issues Two issues dominated the 1984 campaign—the federal **budget deficit** and foreign trade. Reagan and the Republicans played down the deficit, claiming that economic growth, along with budget cuts, would help bring down the deficit. The Republicans also called for reducing **tariffs** to increase foreign trade.

Mondale and the Democrats called for increasing taxes to pay down the deficit. In his nomination acceptance speech, Mondale stated, "Mr. Reagan will raise taxes and so will I. He

Geraldine Ferraro (1935–) married John Zaccaro, a realtor, in 1960 and raised three children. She practice law until 1974 and was then appointed assistant district attorney in Queens, New York. She won elections to the United States House of Representatives in 1978, 1980, and 1982. In her speech accepting the 1984 vice-presidential nomination, she said, "My name is Geraldine Ferraro. I stand before you to proclaim tonight: America is the land where dreams can come true for all of us." She published her autobiography, *Ferraro: My Story*, in 1985. She has remained active in politics and ran unsuccessfully for the United States Senate in 1992 and 1998.

won't tell you. I just did." Mondale gambled that people would respect his honesty. However, the Reagan campaign seized on this statement to run against Mondale as a tax-raiser. The Democrats also called for certain trade restrictions to help protect American businesses.

The Campaign Both candidates and their supporters crossed the nation presenting their views to the voters. Mondale and Ferraro usually spoke to huge crowds but seemed to make little impact on the voters. Reagan remained very popular and criticism did not seem to stick to him. His political opponents called him "The Teflon® President." (Teflon® is a coating applied to pots to keep food from sticking.) His supporters, however, called Reagan "The Great Communicator" because of his ability to reach voters.

Mondale criticized Reagan for wasting money on the development of a nuclear defense program called the Strategic Defense Initiative (SDI). SDI, nicknamed "Star Wars" after a popular science fiction movie, was a space-based system designed to protect the United States from nuclear attack. He pointed out that SDI

Ronald Reagan, known as "The Great Communicator," promised to continue building a proud and vibrant America.

A 1984 Republican campaign button highlights the accomplishments of the Reagan-Bush administration.

was not only expensive but that many scientists believed it would not work.

President Reagan responded that while his tax cuts had caused deficits, they also had stimulated the economy by giving people more money to spend. He claimed that future economic growth would reduce the deficit. Most people also liked the tough stance Reagan took against Communism, particularly against the Soviet Union.

Throughout the campaign, Reagan stressed patriotic themes and family values. One Republican television ad, known as "Morning in America," showed happy, confident people going to work, living full lives, and feeling good about themselves—all against a patriotic background. As Americans went to vote, most were confident in the economy and proud of their nation.

The Election On Election Day, Reagan won a bigger landslide than in the 1980 election. Reagan received 54,400,000 popular votes to Mondale's 37,500,000. The **Electoral College** vote was 525 to 13, as Reagan carried all states except Minnesota and the District of Columbia. *See also* ELECTION OF 1980 (REAGAN); ELECTION OF 1988 (GEORGE H.W. BUSH).

Election of 1988

George H.W. Bush ✪ Bush won a clear victory in 1988 in one of the most negative campaigns in election history.

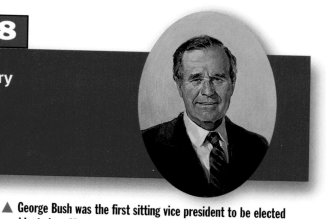

The Candidates George Bush, Ronald Reagan's vice president for eight years, was assured the **Republican** nomination when the convention met in New Orleans. He was nominated on the first **ballot**. For vice president, Bush chose a little-known Indiana senator, James Danforth (Dan) Quayle. Even Republicans, including Bush's closest aides, were surprised at his choice.

Several **Democratic** leaders wanted their party's nomination. Among them were Massachusetts governor Michael S. Dukakis, the Reverend Jesse Jackson, New York governor Mario Cuomo, and former Colorado senator Gary S. Hart. Dukakis quickly won most of the **primary elections**, and his nomination was assured when the Democratic convention met in Atlanta. For vice president, Dukakis selected Texas senator Lloyd

▲ George Bush was the first sitting vice president to be elected president since Martin Van Buren in 1836.

> "Read My Lips, No New Taxes."
> —Republican campaign slogan, 1988

On August 2, 1990, Saddam Hussein, the dictator of Iraq, ordered the invasion of oil-rich Kuwait. In response to this aggression, President Bush, working with the United Nations (UN), put together a coalition of allied nations. These countries imposed a diplomatic and economic boycott of Iraq. At the same time, allied forces took up military positions in Saudi Arabia, Kuwait's neighbor. The Gulf War began on January 17, 1991, with the bombing of Baghdad, the Iraqi capital. Even after five weeks of nonstop bombing, Saddam Hussein would not withdraw Iraqi forces. On February 24, allied forces led by the United States attacked Iraqi troops. The Iraqis surrendered after 100 hours of fighting. After the Gulf War, President Bush's approval rating soared to 89 percent. But as the election of 1992 approached, Bush's popularity suffered, and he was not reelected.

Bentsen.

The Issues The main campaign issue was the huge **budget deficit** that developed under President Reagan. Yet Bush and the Republicans pointed to the successes of the Reagan-Bush administration, citing the healthy economy and the increase in the nation's military strength. In turn, Dukakis and the Democrats claimed that only the wealthy benefited from the Republican's economic policies. The Democrats especially questioned Bush's role in the Iran-Contra affair of the Reagan presidency. This scandal involved members of the Reagan administration selling weapons to Iran in return for the release of American hostages held in the Middle East. The money from the weapons was then used to secretly fund Nicaraguan rebels, known as *contras*.

The Campaign In a nasty campaign, the candidates attacked each other and spent little time discussing the issues or convincing voters that they were the better candidate. Bush accused Dukakis of being unpatriotic and soft on crime.

Barbara Bush (1925–) was born into a well-to-do family. She met George Bush at a dance in 1942, and they became engaged about a year later. Their marriage was delayed when George joined the United States Navy during World War II. The Bushes moved to Texas, where George became successful in the oil business. He then entered politics, and his flourishing career caused them to move to 28 different homes in 17 cities. Barbara believed in volunteering to help others who were less fortunate. She brought this commitment to the White House when she became First Lady. She began the Barbara Bush Foundation for Family Literacy to encourage families to read together. She donated the money from the sale of a book she wrote to the Foundation. The book, titled *Millie's Book*, is the story of life in the White House as told by the First Family's dog, Millie. Barbara Bush also traveled widely as the president's representative and acted as his informal adviser. The Bushes retired to Houston after George lost his reelection bid in 1992. Barbara is the second woman, after Abigail Adams, to be both the wife of a president and the mother of a president—George W. Bush, who was elected in 2000.

The Reverend Jesse Jackson made a strong showing in several primary elections in the 1988 campaign.

He claimed that Dukakis's opposition to certain land-based missiles would threaten the nation's security.

Dukakis questioned Bush's leadership abilities, wondering how the vice president could be unaware of such events as the Iran-Contra scandal. He noted that Bush's first decision as a presidential nominee was choosing the inexperienced Dan Quayle as his running mate, thus further sowing doubts about Bush's leadership. Dukakis vowed to better collect taxes from cheaters—both individuals and businesses—but said he would raise taxes only as a last resort.

In return, Bush pledged never to raise taxes, proclaiming, "Read my lips, no new taxes!" in almost every campaign speech. After the second presidential debate in October, Bush surged ahead in the **polls**.

The Election On Election Day, Bush scored an impressive victory in the **Electoral College**, winning 426 electoral votes to Dukakis's 111. In the popular vote, Bush won about 54 percent to Dukakis's 46 percent. *See also* ELECTION OF 1980 (REAGAN); ELECTION OF 1984 (REAGAN); ELECTION OF 1992 (CLINTON).

Election of 1992

Bill (William Jefferson) Clinton ☻ Clinton was inspired to seek a career in politics when, at age 16, he met President John F. Kennedy. Clinton won the presidency himself at age 47, with less than half of the popular vote in a three-way contest.

▲ Bill Clinton was the first president born after World War II.

The Candidates The **incumbent**, George H.W. Bush, was easily renominated by the **Republican** party. Dan Quayle was again the vice presidential nominee, although some Republican leaders wanted Bush to drop him from the **ticket**. Bush, who had been extremely popular right after the Gulf War (1991), had seen his approval ratings fall as the nation's economy spun into decline.

Several **Democrats** wanted to challenge Bush for the presidency. Among them were Arkansas governor Bill Clinton, former California governor Jerry Brown, and former Massachusetts senator Paul Tsongas. Despite rumors about economic scandals and sexual infidelities, Bill Clinton won most of the Democratic **primary elections** and went on to win the nomination. For vice president, Clinton chose a fellow southerner, Senator Al Gore of Tennessee.

Many voters were displeased with both Bush and Clinton. An independent candidate, Texas billionaire H. Ross Perot, started the **Reform**

> **"It's the economy, stupid!"**
> —Campaign reminder, hanging in candidate Clinton's office, 1992

party and spent millions of dollars of his own on his presidential campaign. For vice president, Perot chose James Stockdale, a retired admiral.

The Issues The major issue of the campaign was the nation's **recession**. Since the end of the Gulf War in 1991, about 2 million people had lost their jobs and health-care costs were rapidly rising.

The Campaign During the campaign Clinton—calling himself a "New Democrat"—promised to restart the economy, balance the budget, and "end welfare as we know it." He supported the death penalty and reached out to minorities and women. He favored the North American Free Trade Agreement (NAFTA), a trade agreement among the United States, Canada, and Mexico.

Bush and the Republicans attacked Clinton's personal integrity, claiming that he

Election of 1992

Candidate (Party)	Popular Vote	Electoral Vote
Bill Clinton (Democrat)	44,909,806	370
George H. W. Bush (Republican)	39,104,550	168
H. Ross Perot (Reform)	19,742,240	0

Hillary Rodham Clinton (1947–   ) was born in the Chicago suburbs. She attended public high school and then studied at Wellesley College in Massachusetts. After graduation, she attended Yale University, earning a law degree in 1973. She met her future husband while at Yale, and they married in 1975. Hillary joined a prominent law firm in Little Rock, Arkansas, and became one of the city's top lawyers. During the 1992 presidential race, she campaigned on behalf of her husband, demonstrating her intelligence and abilities. As First Lady, she sought an active role. The president appointed her to lead a commission to create a health-care reform program, but the plan met with strong opposition from both the public and Congress and was never acted upon. Throughout her eight years as First Lady, Hillary continued to work on behalf of women and children, and she wrote *It Takes a Village*, a book about child rearing. In 1999, the Clintons bought a home in New York, thus enabling Hillary to become a senatorial candidate in New York State. Hillary decisively won the New York senatorial election of 2000, making her the first First Lady to serve in the Senate.

was unpatriotic for not serving in the military during the Vietnam War. They also raised questions about extramarital affairs. Bush, too, supported NAFTA and called for its passage.

Perot focused his campaign on the economy and on the voters' dissatisfaction with government. He promised to lower the federal **budget deficit** and to end the gridlock in Washington that prevented any solutions to the nation's budget issues. Perot opposed NAFTA, claiming it would hurt American workers.

The Election Bill Clinton and the Democrats won the White House after 12 years of Republican control. With a **plurality** of the popular vote, Clinton earned 370 **electoral votes** to Bush's 168. Perot won about 19 percent of the popular vote, but failed to win any electoral votes. *See also* ELECTION OF 1988 (GEORGE H.W. BUSH); ELECTION OF 1996 (CLINTON); ELECTION OF 2000 (GEORGE W. BUSH).

 In 1978, Bill and Hillary Clinton and their friends, James and Susan McDougal, borrowed $203,000 to buy 220 acres of land in Arkansas's Ozark Mountains. They formed a corporation, the Whitewater Development Corporation, hoping to develop the land for vacation homes, but land values plummeted and the group lost money. James McDougal also owned Madison Savings & Loan Association, for which Hillary Clinton did legal work. The Savings & Loan eventually went bankrupt. Some people questioned the legality of certain loans to Clinton associates who were connected to Whitewater. The Clintons maintained their innocence during a long investigation, but James and Susan McDougal were convicted of fraud and conspiracy. Other Clinton associates, including Guy Tucker—who replaced Bill Clinton as governor after the election of 1992—were also found guilty. However, in September 2000, the Whitewater investigation ended. Prosecutors found that there was insufficient evidence to bring any charges against the Clintons.

Election of 1996

Bill (William Jefferson) Clinton ☉ Despite ongoing controversy, Clinton easily won reelection in 1996. He was the first Democrat reelected to a second full term since Franklin D. Roosevelt in 1936.

The Candidates The **Democrats** easily nominated the popular Bill Clinton for a second term. Vice President Al Gore was again his running mate.

The **Republicans** chose Senator Bob Dole of Kansas as their nominee. As the majority leader in the Senate, Dole had a great deal of government experience. For vice president, the Republicans selected former congressman Jack Kemp, a popular conservative from New York.

Reform party candidate H. Ross Perot also ran again. His vice presidential nominee was Pat Choate, an influential economist. Perot and Choate were both opposed to **free trade**.

The Issues As in the past two elections, economic issues again played a role in the campaign, even though the nation's economy was growing rapidly. The candidates also focused on domestic issues such as crime, television violence,

▲ Bill Clinton was the second president in the nation's history to be impeached.

- ● "The
- ● Comeback
- ● Kid"
- ● —*Nickname for Bill Clinton*

and teen smoking. Both parties promised to improve America's moral values.

The Campaign Clinton and Gore took credit for the country's economic prosperity. They claimed that Dole and the Republicans favored the wealthy and wanted to eliminate Medicare. Dole promised a 15 percent tax cut. He tried to portray Clinton as a tax-and-spend **liberal** who was out of touch with most voters.

Although throughout the campaign, the Republicans and Perot's Reform party raised questions about President Clinton's business ethics and his private behavior, Clinton maintained a large lead in the polls. A booming economy, low inflation, and low unemployment helped the president's image. In late 1996, Clinton

Al Gore (1948–) was born in Washington, D.C. His father, Albert Gore, Sr., served in the House of Representatives for 14 years and then in the Senate for three terms. The younger Gore grew up in Washington and attended school there but spent his summers working on the family farm in Carthage, Tennessee. In 1976, Gore won his father's seat in the House of Representatives and went on to the Senate in 1984. During his years in Congress, he became an expert on the environment and technology. Bill Clinton chose Gore, a moderate liberal, to be his running mate in 1992 and again in 1996. After eight years as vice president, Al Gore ran for the presidency in 2000 but was defeated by George W. Bush in one of the closest elections in American history.

Election of 1996

Candidate (Party)	Popular Vote	Electoral Vote
Bill Clinton (Democrat)	47,402,357	379
Robert Dole (Republican)	39,198,755	159
H. Ross Perot (Reform)	8,085,402	0

signed a welfare reform bill, which was popular with many people. In addition, many voters believed that Republicans had pushed too hard for their conservative policies. Voters also blamed the Republicans for twice shutting down the government during a 1995 budget crisis.

During his first term, the president also enjoyed a successful foreign policy. He advanced peace in the Middle East and in Ireland. Clinton expanded humanitarian programs and peacefully reestablished an elected government in the poverty-stricken nation of Haiti. His biggest success was a complex peace treaty, signed in Dayton, Ohio, ending a civil war in the European nation of Bosnia. Clinton then sent American troops, as part of a NATO force, to help keep the peace in Bosnia.

It seemed that most voters were relatively happy with the condition of the country. The nation was at peace, jobs were available, and the crime rate was down. As the election approached, voters supported the president and his policies.

Near the end of the campaign, Dole asked Perot to drop out of the race and endorse him, rather than allow Clinton to win reelection. But Perot stayed in the running.

Impeachment is the formal accusation of wrongdoing by a government official. In American history, only two presidents have been impeached—Andrew Johnson in 1868 and Bill Clinton in 1998. In both instances, the House of Representatives passed articles of impeachment, citing formal charges of the alleged offenses. The Senate then tried the case against the president, and the chief justice of the United States presided over the trial. Both presidents were found not guilty and served the remainder of their terms.

Clinton's presidency was surrounded by rumors of economic scandal and sexual misconduct. United States Attorney General Janet Reno appointed several special prosecutors to investigate the charges. Finally in 1998, special prosecutor Kenneth Starr presented his report to the House of Representatives, charging that Clinton had obstructed justice, abused his power as president, and committed perjury. On December 19, 1998, the House passed two articles of impeachment, citing perjury and obstruction of justice. The case then moved to the Senate for trial. Chief Justice William H. Rehnquist presided. On February 12, 1999, the Senate voted to acquit the president. Although Clinton remained in office, his reputation had suffered.

The Election On Election Day, Clinton scored a huge victory in the **Electoral College**—379 **electoral votes** to Dole's 159. As in 1992, H. Ross Perot did not win any electoral votes. *See also* ELECTION OF 1992 (CLINTON); ELECTION OF 2000 (GEORGE W. BUSH).

Election of 2000

George W. Bush ✪ Bush lost the popular vote but won the election in the Electoral College in one of the closest elections in the nation's history.

The Candidates After the **Republican** defeat in the ELECTION OF 1996, many party leaders rallied around George W. Bush, the governor of Texas and the son of former president George H.W. Bush. They believed that he would be a strong presidential candidate. Other Republicans also sought the nomination, including Arizona senator John McCain and the owner of *Forbes* magazine, Steve Forbes. During the **primary elections**, Bush and McCain became the **front-runners**. Bush easily won the nomination at the Republican convention. For vice president, Bush chose Richard B. (Dick) Cheney, a former congressman from Wyoming and secretary of defense.

The **Democrats** nominated Vice President Al Gore for president. For vice president, Gore chose Connecticut senator Joseph Lieberman, the first Jewish American on a major party **ticket**.

Dissatisfied with both major party nominees, Ralph Nader ran as the candidate of the **Green party**. Nader, a consumer advocate and environmentalist, chose as his running mate Winona LaDuke, a political and environmental activist of the Chippewa in northern Minnesota.

The Issues A major issue of the campaign centered on what to do with **surplus** tax revenues. The Republicans wanted a large tax cut. The Democrats favored a smaller tax cut, holding the remaining money to ensure support for

> •
> • **"I was not**
> • **elected to**
> • **serve one**
> • **party, but to**
> • **serve one**
> • **nation."**
> •
> • —*George W. Bush, televised*
> • *statement, December 13, 2000*

▲ George W. Bush and John Quincy Adams are the only U.S. presidents whose father was also president.

Social Security and to pay down the national deficit. Both major parties supported education reform and plans that would help older Americans pay for prescription drugs.

The Campaign Calling himself a "compassionate **conservative**," Bush tried to appeal to a wide range of voters. He spoke out for a large tax cut, preserving Social Security, and improving education. He criticized President Clinton's personal behavior of the past eight years, stressing that he would restore "honor and decency" to the White House.

Gore prohibited President Clinton from campaigning on his behalf. He and the Democrats took credit for the strong economy, citing the nation's growing prosperity. Gore called for the Environmental Protection Agency (EPA) to strictly enforce cleanup laws.

Nader argued that there was little difference between the two major candidates. He claimed that because both Bush and Gore were dependent on campaign donations from America's big corporations, neither candidate was supporting the country's workers. He also favored environmental protections and national health care.

The Election The race appeared close as the votes were being counted the evening of Election Day. The media first declared Gore the winner, claiming he had won the 25 **electoral votes** of Florida. Later the media retracted its assessment and declared Bush the winner. By the early morning hours of November 8, the election was undecided. The outcome would remain uncertain for 36 days.

The popular vote in Florida was so close—a few hundred votes apart—that state law called for a recount of the votes. In Florida most voters cast their vote by punching a small hole in a ballot. The tiny piece of cardboard that is punched out is called a **chad**. On some ballots the chad was still hanging by one or two corners, rather than being completely removed from the ballot. Controversy raged because the vote counters were determining the voter's intention, even when the chad was still attached. In addition, some leaders claimed that in a few Florida counties African Americans were kept from voting because their names were illegally removed from voter lists or they were simply turned away from voting booths.

A series of lawsuits and countersuits began. Under Florida law, officials are required to certify the vote by a certain date. When it appeared that all the manual recounts would not be completed in time, Gore went to court to have the deadline extended. Then Bush requested that the United States Supreme Court determine if the Florida court had acted unconstitutionally by extending the deadline.

The vote counting continued but was still unfinished by the new deadline. On November 27, Florida officials certified Bush as the winner by 537 votes. Gore's attorneys headed back to court, arguing that thousands of ballots were still uncounted. The Florida Supreme Court called for another manual recount of the votes in all Florida counties. Counting began, but the United States Supreme Court ordered the counting to stop until it had issued its ruling.

On December 12, in the case *Bush v. Gore*, the United States Supreme Court ruled that the hand recounts in Florida violated the equal protection clause of the Constitution. The court noted that because the vote counters used different standards, the recount did not treat all voters equally. The court went on to rule that the manual recount could not be completed in time to meet the date required by the Constitution to count the electoral votes. This ruling left Bush as the certified winner in Florida, thus awarding him the presidency. The next day, Gore conceded the election in a televised speech. Bush responded, calling for national unity.

The final electoral vote was 271 for Bush and 266 for Gore. Nationwide, however, Gore had won more popular votes than Bush. Bush is the fourth president to win the electoral vote but lose the popular vote, the others being John Quincy Adams (1824), Rutherford B. Hayes (1877), and Benjamin Harrison (1888). *See also* ELECTION OF 1996 (CLINTON).

Laura Bush (1946–) was born into a middle-class family in Midland, Texas. After attending public school, she enrolled in Southern Methodist University and graduated with an education degree in 1968. She taught school and went on to earn a master's degree in library science from the University of Texas. She met George W. Bush through mutual friends and they married in 1977. When George was governor of Texas, Laura organized the Texas Book Festival to raise money for the state's libraries and she helped raise literacy awareness. As First Lady, Laura Bush continued to work to improve education.

Selected Bibliography

Barone, Michael. *Our Country: The Shaping of America from Roosevelt to Reagan.* New York: The Free Press, 1990.

Boller, Paul F. *Presidential Campaigns.* New York: Oxford University Press, 1984.

Boller, Paul F. *Presidential Inaugurations.* New York: Harcourt, 2001.

Boller, Paul F. *Presidential Wives.* New York: Oxford University Press, 1988.

Bralier, Jess, and Sally Chabert. *Presidential Wit and Wisdom.* New York: Penguin Books, 1996.

Brinkley, Alan, and Ted Widmer. *Campaigns: A Century of Presidential Races.* New York: Dorling and Kindersley, 2001.

Caroli, Betty Boyd. *First Ladies.* New York: Oxford University Press, 1995.

DeGregorio, William A. *The Complete Book of U.S. Presidents.* New York: Wings Books, 1991.

Donald, David Herbert. *Lincoln.* New York: Simon & Schuster, 1995.

Ellis, Joseph J. *Founding Brothers.* New York: Alfred A. Knopf, 2001.

Kane, Joseph Nathan. *Presidential Fact Book.* New York: Random House, 1999.

Kunhardt, Philip B., Jr., et al. *The American President.* New York: Riverhead Books, 1999.

McCullough, David. *John Adams.* New York: Simon & Schuster, 2001.

McPherson, James M., ed. *To the Best of My Ability: The American Presidents.* New York: Dorling Kindersley, 2000.

Purcell, Edward L., ed. *Vice Presidents: A Biographical Dictionary.* New York: Checkmark Books, 2001.

Salinger, Pierre. *John F. Kennedy: Commander in Chief.* New York: Gramercy Books, 1997.

Rehnquist, William H. *Grand Inquests: The Historic Impeachments of Justice Samuel Chase and President Andrew Johnson.* New York: Morrow, 1999.

Rubel, David. *Mr. President: The Human Side of America's Chief Executives.* Alexandria, Virginia: Time-Life Books, 1998.

Sidey, Hugh. *Hugh Sidey's Profiles of the Presidents.* Boston: Little, Brown and Co., 2000.

Tally, Steve. *Bland Ambition.* Orlando: Harcourt, Brace, Jovanovich, 1992.

Whalen, Richard, and Evan Comog. *Hats in the Ring: An Illustrated History of American Presidential Elections.* New York: Random House, 2000.

Witcover, Jules. *Crapshoot: Rolling the Dice on the Vice Presidency.* New York: Crown Publishers, 1992.

Selected Web Sites

America Votes: Presidential Campaign Memorabilia
http://scriptorium.lib.duke.edu/americavotes

The American Presidency: A Glorious Burden
http://americanhistory.si.edu/presidency/home.html

The Closest Presidential Races
http://www.infoplease.com/spot/closerace1.html

Dave Leip's Atlas of U.S. Presidential Elections
http://uselectionatlas.org

LIFE at the Conventions, 1948–1996
http://www.life.com/Life/conventions

Parades, Protests, Politics: Chicago's Political Conventions
http://www.chicagohs.org/P3/PolCon.html

The Times Looks Back: Presidential Elections 1896–1996
http://www.nytimes.com/learning/general/specials/elections/

U.S. Elections
http://www.infoplease.com/ipa/A0764586.html

U.S. Presidential Election Maps: 1860–1996
http://fisher.lib.virginia.edu/elections/maps

Facts About the Presidents

President	Born-Died	Term of Office	Party	State	Vice President(s)
1. George Washington	1732–1799	1789–1797	None	Virginia	John Adams
2. John Adams	1735–1826	1797–1801	Federalist	Massachusetts	Thomas Jefferson
3. Thomas Jefferson	1743–1826	1801-1809	Democratic-Republican	Virginia	Aaron Burr George Clinton
4. James Madison	1751–1836	1809–1817	Democratic-Republican	Virginia	George Clinton Elbridge Gerry
5. James Monroe	1758–1831	1817–1825	Democratic-Republican	Virginia	Daniel D. Tompkins
6. John Quincy Adams	1767–1848	1825–1829	Democratic-Republican	Massachusetts	John C. Calhoun
7. Andrew Jackson	1767–1845	1829–1837	Democratic	Tennessee	John C. Calhoun Martin Van Buren
8. Martin Van Buren	1782–1862	1837–1841	Democratic	New York	Richard M. Johnson
9. William Henry Harrison*	1773–1841	1841 (1 month)	Whig	Ohio	John Tyler
10. John Tyler	1790–1862	1841–1845	Whig	Virginia	
11. James K. Polk	1795–1849	1845–1849	Democratic	Tennessee	George M. Dallas
12. Zachary Taylor*	1784–1850	1849–1850	Whig	Louisiana	Millard Fillmore
13. Millard Fillmore	1800–1874	1850–1853	Whig	New York	
14. Franklin Pierce	1804–1869	1853–1857	Democratic	New Hampshire	William R. King
15. James Buchanan	1791–1868	1857–1861	Democratic	Pennsylvania	John C. Breckinridge
16. Abraham Lincoln+	1809–1865	1861–1865	Republican	Illinois	Hannibal Hamlin Andrew Johnson
17. Andrew Johnson	1808–1875	1865–1869	Democratic**	Tennessee	
18. Ulysses S. Grant	1822–1885	1869–1877	Republican	Illinois	Schuyler Colfax Henry Wilson
19. Rutherford B. Hayes	1822–1893	1877–1881	Republican	Ohio	William A. Wheeler
20. James A. Garfield+	1831–1881	1881	Republican	Ohio	Chester A. Arthur
21. Chester A. Arthur	1829–1886	1881–1885	Republican	New York	
22. Grover Cleveland	1837–1908	1885–1889	Democratic	New York	Thomas A. Hendricks
23. Benjamin Harrison	1833–1901	1889–1893	Republican	Ohio	Levi P. Morton
24. Grover Cleveland	1837–1908	1893–1897	Democratic	New York	Adlai E. Stevenson

continued

Facts About the Presidents—*Continued*

President	Born-Died	Term of Office	Party	State	Vice President(s)
25. William McKinley+	1843–1901	1897–1901	Republican	Ohio	Garret A. Hobart Theodore Roosevelt
26. Theodore Roosevelt	1858–1919	1901–1909	Republican	New York	Charles W. Fairbanks
27. William H. Taft	1857–1930	1909–1913	Republican	Ohio	James S. Sherman
28. Woodrow Wilson	1856–1924	1913–1921	Democratic	New Jersey	Thomas R. Marshall
29. Warren G. Harding*	1865–1923	1921–1923	Republican	Ohio	Calvin Coolidge
30. Calvin Coolidge	1872–1933	1923–1929	Republican	Massachusetts	Charles G. Dawes
31. Herbert C. Hoover	1874–1964	1929–1933	Republican	California	Charles Curtis
32. Franklin D. Roosevelt*	1882–1945	1933–1945	Democratic	New York	John Nance Garner Henry A. Wallace Harry S. Truman
33. Harry S. Truman	1884–1972	1945–1953	Democratic	Missouri	Alben W. Barkley
34. Dwight D. Eisenhower	1890–1969	1953–1961	Republican	New York	Richard M. Nixon
35. John F. Kennedy+	1917–1963	1961–1963	Democratic	Massachusetts	Lyndon B. Johnson
36. Lyndon B. Johnson	1908–1973	1963–1969	Democratic	Texas	Hubert H. Humphrey
37. Richard M. Nixon++	1913–1994	1969–1974	Republican	California	Spiro T. Agnew Gerald R. Ford
38. Gerald R. Ford	1913–	1974–1977	Republican	Michigan	Nelson A. Rockefeller
39. Jimmy (James Earl) Carter	1924–	1977–1981	Democratic	Georgia	Walter F. Mondale
40. Ronald W. Reagan	1911–	1981–1989	Republican	California	George H.W. Bush
41. George H.W. Bush	1924–	1989–1993	Republican	Texas	J. Danforth Quayle
42. Bill (William) J. Clinton	1946–	1993–2001	Democratic	Arkansas	Albert S. Gore
43. George W. Bush	1946–	2001–	Republican	Texas	Richard B. Cheney

*Died while in office

+Assassinated while in office

**Democrat Andrew Johnson ran with Republican Abraham Lincoln on the National Union ticket.

++Resigned

Theodore Roosevelt, who took office at age 42, was the youngest president. Ronald Reagan, who took office at 69, was the oldest. Although neither race, religion, nor gender is a requirement for the office, all presidents so far have been white men. Only one president was Roman Catholic—John F. Kennedy. However, in recent years, Elizabeth Dole, a woman, and Jesse Jackson, an African American, made serious runs for the presidency, and Joseph Lieberman, who is Jewish, ran for vice president.

abolition: the social movement before the Civil War (1861–1865) that demanded an end to slavery

abolitionists: members of the movement advocating the end of slavery

acclamation: an affirmative vote expressed by cheers and shouts rather than by ballot

American Independent party: a political party founded by Alabama governor George Wallace in 1968; the party supported states' rights and segregation

amnesty: an official pardon, usually granted by a government or military official

anarchist: a person who rebels against authority or ruling power, usually by advocating the overthrow of those powers

annexation: the act of incorporating a territory within a state or country

Anti-Federalists: a group that opposed the adoption of the United States Constitution

Articles of Confederation: the first plan of government of the United States, in effect from 1781 to 1789

balanced federal budget: a budget plan in which the government's income is equal to its spending

ballot: a round of voting; also, the actual form on which an individual's vote is cast

Bill of Rights: the first ten amendments to the United States Constitution, which guarantee individual rights and freedoms

bosses: during the mid-1800s to the early 1900s, political leaders who controlled several state and local governments by awarding jobs and political favors in return for votes

broadside: a small poster printed on one side, which often announced political news

budget deficit: a budget situation in which the government spends more money than it collects

caucus: a closed meeting of political leaders in which they choose a candidate or decide on a policy

chad: a very small piece of cardboard punched out of a voting card

collective bargaining: the negotiations between an employer and a union to agree on the working conditions (wages, hours, benefits, etc.) of employees

compromise candidate: a person who is chosen to run for office because he or she is acceptable to opposing groups, or factions, within a political party

conservative: a person who generally supports traditional norms, views, or institutions

Constitutional Union party: a political party, organized in 1860, that tried to preserve the Union at the outbreak of the Civil War (1861–1865)

convention: a meeting of political party members to select candidates for office

dark horse: a relatively unknown political candidate

deadlocked: a situation in which there appears to be no agreement

Democratic party: one of the two major political parties in the United States today. (Members of the Democratic party are **Democrats.**)

Democratic-Republicans: a political party of the early 1800s that tried to restrict the powers of the federal government and expand the powers and rights of the states

depression: a period of low economic activity, usually indicated by high unemployment rates

Dixiecrats: a political party organized in 1948 by the conservative Southern faction of the Democratic party because they opposed the party's stand on civil rights for African Americans

draft: non-voluntary selection for military service

Electoral College: in the United States, the body of men and women elected by the voters that in turn chooses the president and vice president by majority vote

electoral vote: the vote cast for president and vice president by a member of the Electoral College

embargo: a government order preventing specific types of trade with a foreign country

excise tax: a tax on the sale or manufacture of goods within a country

faction: a subgroup of a political party

Federalists: in late 1700s and early 1800s, a political party that favored a strong central government

free trade: the exchange of goods with no tariffs or restrictions

front-runner: the apparent leading candidate or the party favorite

graft: to gain money in illegal or questionable ways

Green party: a political party founded in the 1980s to focus awareness on environmental and equity issues

impeachment: the formal accusation of a government official of wrongdoing; the first step in removing that person from office

impressment: the act of forcing American sailors to serve in the British navy, in common practice from about 1790 to 1812

inauguration: the swearing in of a government official

incumbent: the person currently holding office

inflation: an economic situation in which prices tend to rise but income remains constant

integration: unrestricted mixing of different ethnic groups

isolationist: a person who advocates a foreign policy that has little to do with other nations

League of Nations: a multinational organization founded in 1919, after World War I, to help solve international problems and keep world peace

liberal: a person who advocates change or reform

majority: the greater number or more than one-half

monarchy: a country ruled by a king or a queen

monopolies: businesses in which there is no competition

mudslinging: a campaign tactic in which often untrue stories, or "political dirt," are told about an opponent

nationalism: a feeling of pride in and loyalty to one's home country

National Republicans: party name used by John Quincy Adams and his supporters in the election of 1828

neutrality: not taking sides

platform: the official views of a political party stated before an election

plurality: the greatest number of votes, but not more than one-half of the whole number of votes cast

political party: an organization of people who join together to win elections, control government, and determine public policy

polls: surveys conducted before an election to determine how the candidates are faring in the race

popular sovereignty: the concept that the people hold final governmental authority

popular vote: the total number of ballots cast by the people

press: the mass media, especially newspapers and magazines

primary elections: elections held to decide the party's nominees for office

progressive: people who wanted social, economic, and governmental reforms, especially in the late 1800s and early 1900s

Progressive party: a political party that favored social, economic, and governmental reforms

Prohibition: the practice of forbidding the production, transportation, or sale of alcoholic beverages

ratify: to approve (an amendment or treaty)

recession: a situation in which the economy slows down and some people lose their jobs

reform: to put an end to governmental faults or abuses by introducing a better course of action

Reform party: a political party founded by millionaire H. Ross Perot in 1992; the party opposed free trade and supported paying the national debt

repeal: to revoke a law so that it is no longer in effect

Republican party: one of the two major political parties in the United States today. (Members of the Republican party are **Republicans.**)

secede: to withdraw from the Union

segregation: the practice of separating racial or ethnic groups

smear tactics: lies or exaggerations designed to ruin a candidate's reputation and prevent voters from supporting him or her

spoils system: the practice of appointing members of the winner's political party to office

states' rights: the theory that state law overrides federal law

surplus: an extra amount

tariff: a tax imposed by the government, especially on imported goods

third party: in the United States, any political party other than the Republican party and the Democratic party

ticket: the list of candidates of the same political party up for election

Whigs: members of a political party in the United States from about the 1830s to 1860

Page numbers for the subjects of feature boxes are in boldface. Page numbers for illustrations are in italics.